Penny Candy

Penny Candy

JEAN KERR

Illustrations by Whitney Darrow, Jr.

DOUBLEDAY & COMPANY, INC.
GARDEN CITY, NEW YORK

Contents

The pieces in this book have appeared in the following magazines:

"Marriage: Unsafe at Any Speed" and "The Words That Come Before the Music" (under the title "How Charming, Intelligent Women Drive Their Husbands Crazy") in *Family Circle*.

"I Don't Want to See the Uncut Version of *Anything*" in *Dramatists' Guild Bulletin*.

"I Saw Mommy Kicking Santa Claus," "What to Do When Your Husband Gives Up Smoking," "Why Mommy Can't Read," "Twiggy Who?" and "The Poet and the Peasants" in *McCall's* magazine.

"Confessions of a Sea-lubber" in *Holiday*.

"I Just Stepped Out of *Vogue*," "How to Talk to a Baby," "As I Was Saying to a Geranium," "Partying Is Such Sweet Sorrow" and "The Children's Hour After Hour After Hour" in *Ladies' Home Journal*.

"My Twenty-one Minute Shape-up Program" in *Vogue*.

FOR RICHARD WATTS, JR.

Penny Candy

Introduction

The mail I get is mysterious at best. When I tell you that our children, who, I'm afraid, have been overexposed to whimsy, frequently send us letters from school addressed to "Occupant, One Beach Avenue, Larchmont, New York," and that these often represent the high point of the morning's catch, you will understand why we are held in such low regard by our postman. This same postman is additionally harassed because he has to ring twice and sometimes thrice to collect the postage due on three of the four copies of *The New Republic* we receive every week. (The older boys change their addresses so often, what with their winter classes, their summer classes, their time at home and their temporary employment, that I imagine *The New Republic* believes them to be on the lam and feels that any effort to make direct contact with them should be left to the FBI.)

I also receive chance-books for the benefit of the Don Bosco Guild and mimeographed bulletins from Gristede's when their canned tomatoes are on sale. And, of course, I get bills—with enclosures. In this connection I must say that I think it is awfully sweet of Saks Fifth Avenue to keep sending me enclosures even though I no longer get bills (I just don't shop in the city any more, that's all). Saks keeps me in mind. Every time they launch a new line of cosmetics I get two ounces of mail on the subject. It is perhaps significant to mention that they never pursue me in connection with their new swim suits. Somebody there must know me. Anyway, today I learned of a new bath oil of such charismatic power that I gather it would turn my husband into a ravening beast and cause strangers to ogle me in elevators. But I'm afraid it's all too late. It's so long ago now that I don't think I'd recognize an ogle if I saw one.

Also, I hear from my readers. I don't think I am exaggerating when I tell you that I get as much as a trickle of mail from my readers. There is only one thing odd about it. My readers, it would appear (no sampling is totally accurate), are all either post-operatives or pre-teens.

The post-operatives have assured me that my books are welcome because their lack of bulk makes them easy to hold on new incisions without risk to the sutures. (This advantage is not to be sneered at. I myself—after an operation—made the nearly fatal mistake of trying to hoist

The Collected Novels of Collette, which for ease and convenience had been put into one volume.)

Speaking of ailing readers, I got a really heartrending letter from a lady in a Philadelphia hospital who was recovering from an appendectomy. She liked the book all right, but she had received three copies from well-intentioned friends and she wanted to know if I was prepared to buy two of them back. Now, I'll do almost anything for a bona-fide reader, but I must confess this put me in a real spot. What she didn't know, and what perhaps you don't know, is that the publisher *gives* every writer six copies of a book when it is published, to get the ball rolling as it were, and, after you have presented one copy to your mother and one each to your two brothers, you still have three copies going a-begging. I don't really like to give copies of a book to friends because that seems to require them to read it, or at least to pretend to read it. (A truly diplomatic friend of mine solved that problem by writing "Jean, your book is here and looks absolutely delicious. I am saving it until Ted takes his sabbatical.") What I want to say to that lady in Philadelphia is this: we are all mortal, and if she will just sit tight, sooner or later two of her friends will come down with babies or the Hong Kong flu, and *then* she can unload.

The reason I'm certain that the rest of my readers are not yet adolescent is that they announce their age in the very first sentence: "I am a boy of eleven and I liked your book—Billy Phelps" or "I am in fifth grade and I liked your book—Johnny Davis." What I am waiting for is a letter that reads "I am a boy of forty-four and I liked your book—Paul Newman." (Dreams, idle dreams, I know not what they mean.)

Now, what all of this is leading up to is the fact that, when I am hunting for a title for a new book, I do try to think of possible readers. (I must conclude that the old ones have recovered and/or grown up and are now reading Toynbee's A *Study of History*. Well, never mind. Life goes on and there's an eleven-year-old born every minute.) With a novel, or what my children call a *real* book, the problem is simple. If the story is about a man who is called Uncle Tom and who lives in a cabin, any fool could come up with a title. But when the book is a collection of short pieces, the problem is more complex. Let me tell you about two titles I allowed myself to be talked out of.

The woman who lives exactly next door to me has an enchanting assortment of tiny grandchildren, all of whom look and behave as if they were friends of Charlie Brown. One Sunday morning I was driving to church and noticed a tow-headed infant (about two) running along the low wall that edges their property. The snappers in his corduroy overalls had become unsnapped and the legs of the pants were flapping out behind him. He was holding his fat little hands high in the air, reaching out, and he was calling something. I couldn't see any sign of a ball, but I slowed down to hear what he was saying. What he was saying was, "Wait for me, butterfly!"

That lifted my spirits for a whole day. I also thought it might be a title. So I suggested it to my oldest son, who ruminated, "*Wait for Me, Butterfly?* That sounds like a sad novel about a brave girl who recovers from an attack of polio." I don't know why I talk to him anyway.

The other idea for a title came to me when we attended our Kitty's first dancing recital. She was four and wore a costume of red velvet and pink tulle so elaborate that it required three fittings (I had *one* fitting for my wedding gown). The little tag pinned on her costume read "*Cardinal.*" I questioned my husband: "I suppose that means she is a bird?" He replied (typically), "I doubt that she's an ecclesiastic."

In any case, the hall was filled, the program about to start, when a man came slowly from behind the curtain to make an announcement on behalf of the management. Long years in the theater, and the expression on the man's face, made it clear that we were in for a disappointment. And so we were. He cleared his throat several times, then said mournfully, "I am very sorry to tell you that we are missing one Bluejay due to chicken pox."

This time I checked the title with a friend. "What does this mean to you," I asked, "*We Are Missing One Bluejay.*" His answer was brief. "It means you are against air pollution." Of course, I *am* against air pollution, but I am hardly equipped to write about it.

I might never have found a title for this book at all if I hadn't been working on a crossword puzzle. The clue was "assorted trifles," and the answer—17 across—contained ten letters. I never did figure it out, but the solution appeared on the following Sunday—Penny candy. I went back to my friend who was so alert about the pollution problem. "What does *this* title make you think of?" I asked—*"Penny Candy."* His face lit up like a lantern. *"Penny Candy,"* he repeated after me, savoring each forgotten syllable. "Penny candy is Mary Janes, and green leaves, and sour balls and chocolate pigs and licorice whips and red half-dollars and golf-ball lollipops and . . ."

"That's okay," I said. At least I *think* it's okay.

I just stepped out of *Vogue*

Last spring I saw a play called *And Things That Go Bump in the Night*. I won't tell you the plot. But it was about this young man who was so disturbed that he turned up in the second act wearing a dress.

I don't know what he was disturbed about. But I know what I was disturbed about. He was wearing my dress. I mean the one I had on. There it was, the same check, the same little pique collar, the same dreary buttons down the front. Except for the fact that I wear my hair shorter and I'm getting quite gray, we could have been twins.

My first instinct was to flee the premises immediately, perhaps on the pretext that I was suffering appendicitis pains. (After all, it is not widely known that I have already parted with my appendix.) But it occurred to me that if I dashed up the center aisle looking precisely like the leading man I might be regarded as part of the entertainment. So I just slouched down into my seat and pressed my purse up under my chin in the hope of covering at least the collar of that wretched dress. Thereafter I just waited until the entire audience had dispersed before I crept out under cover of darkness.

The incident left its mark on me. But it did serve to clear up an episode that had always been something of a mystery. Two years earlier I had been standing in the lobby of a hotel in Venice. Right next to me, waiting for her key, was a woman I recognized as the celebrated couturier Valentina. I noticed that she was looking exquisite in beige linen. I also noticed that she was staring at me in some perplexity. It was as though she were mentally snapping her fingers.

Thinking I understood the situation, I said, "Madame Valentina, we've never met, but my husband reviews plays and I see you very often at opening nights." And I told her my name. She smiled, and said very quietly, "Oh, I *knew* the name."

I didn't have the wit, or perhaps I didn't have the heart, to ask the next question: "What didn't you know?" So we bowed and parted gravely. Of course, it's all clear enough to me now. I was wearing that same damn brown check dress, with—oh, my God—blue tennis shoes. And Madame Valentina was asking herself "Where did she buy it? When? Why?"

Well, that's what happens when you try to hobnob. As for that particular dress, I have already taken a garden

rake and some matches and burned it in the driveway. But the question remains: Why *do* I have all these horrible golfing-type dresses when, for one thing, I don't even golf? It's true that I am tall and hard to fit, but I don't think the salesladies I get even try. At the first sight of me they smile wanly (as though greeting the recently bereaved), waggle their heads and say, "Oh, I'm afraid I wouldn't have a thing."

Now how can they tell that when I haven't even taken off my coat? Eventually, they brighten up just enough to ask, "Has Madam tried our sports-wear section?" Passing the buck is what I call it. Anyway, that's my problem. I've been trying the sports-wear section for twenty years.

Other women arrange their wardrobes with such *élan*. I have read that Mrs. Michelene Lerner keeps life-sized foam-rubber models of her figure in various fashion houses in Rome, Paris, London, and New York. Then, if she sees a picture of a dress she admires, she doesn't even have to go in for a fitting. She can just call London or Paris and order it. I think this is a marvelous plan. And the reason I haven't had a dozen foam-rubber models made of my figure is not just that there isn't enough foam-rubber in the world. The real reason I'm hesitant is that I don't think a life-sized foam-rubber model of me could be stashed away in a closet someplace, between fittings. It would absolutely require a proper setting. It would have to be placed like Michelangelo's David—in a rotunda, with perhaps a skylight. Now, I have never been in a fashion house but I doubt if they have rotundas. Also, I have the feeling that it would be rather depressing to have oneself duplicated all over the place. Imagine trying to eat some *crème-brûlée* and realizing that you were getting fat in four different cities.

Mignon McLaughlin has written that a woman can remember exactly what she was wearing on every important occasion of her life. I believe that. I can remember. I just wish I could forget. Because even when I find a dress that is pretty and becoming, it turns out, in one way or another, to be a mistake. Let me give you a typical example.

Years ago, when my husband first went to work on a newspaper, we were invited to a dinner party by the man who was then the managing editor. Now I didn't really suppose my husband would be fired if I should prove unsuitable (I don't think newspapers worry about their "image" the way corporations do) but I did suppose that

I couldn't appear at a chic dinner party in a dress that buttoned down the front. I knew I had to take steps.

I went to Lord & Taylor and bravely marched into "Better Dresses." Then I stood in a corner for a while and studied the salesladies. What I did *not* want was an elegant saleslady. I knew, from past experience, that in the presence of a really elegant saleslady with a really elegant European accent I tend to drop my purse and my gloves and to develop coughing spells.

I finally selected one who seemed a little shy and nervous. I went over to her and took hold of her elbow. "Don't *argue* with me," I said, "I want to buy a dress. I want to buy a fancy dress. And I want to buy it this afternoon." She didn't seem startled by my outburst. She just sighed a little sigh that seemed to say "Boy, I get all the nuts!" Then she went to work and found me a pretty dress. It was made of yellow silk pongee with metallic gold thread woven through the fabric. And so I went to the party calm in my conviction that for once I was wearing something that did not look as though it had been run up by loving hands at home.

My husband and I were the first to arrive because we had made the youthful error of arriving at precisely the time for which we had been invited. The editor and his wife greeted us in the foyer and were most gracious. I felt, however, that the wife's smile was a little bit strained. I understood everything when we walked into the living room. Three walls of the room were covered from floor to ceiling with draperies. And the draperies were made of exactly the same material as my new dress. What depressed me most was my feeling that I *wouldn't* die of embarrassment.

I tried to appraise the over-all situation. It wasn't so terrible. It just looked as though they'd had enough material left over to make a dress. But then why, in heaven's name, would I be wearing it? Actually, it didn't matter so much to me that when I was standing in front of a drapery I seemed to be a disembodied head. It mattered more to the other guests, who were hard put to analyze what they assumed must be an optical illusion. Conversations with me had a way of sputtering out. In fact, one man left my side in the middle of a sentence muttering, "I don't know *what* they put in this drink." Finally, I had to devote all of my energies to keeping near the one undraped—or safe—wall, where the heat from the open fireplace promptly took the curl out of my hair. Needless to say, we were not invited back.

Another reason I have so many dreary dresses is that I *know* I am a difficult size, which means that whenever a saleslady produces a dress that actually fits me I feel a sporting obligation to buy it. (I consider a dress fits me when it reaches to my knees and can be zipped up by only one person.) I seem unable to make plain statements like "I can't wear beige because I *am* beige." I may venture a feeble question, "Don't you think it's a little on the beige side?", but if I do the saleslady instantly counters with "Madam must imagine it dressed up with spanking white accessories." So naturally I buy the dress. I'm certainly not going to confess to that girl that I don't own one single spanking white accessory.

By contrast, my mother has great authority in these situations. I once went shopping with her when she was looking for a dress to wear to my brother's wedding. The saleslady brought out a somber mauve lace with that ubiquitous rhinestone pin on the hip. Mother waved it away. The saleslady turned frosty on the instant and asked, "Would you care to tell me what you don't like about it?" Mother smiled cheerily and said, "My dear, all my friends are being *buried* in that dress." She got results, and a very becoming grey chiffon, in ten minutes.

There is this to be said for my ill-purchased dresses. They are, almost invariably, of such stout material and such sturdy construction that it gives me a very good feeling when I pack them off to the Clothes for Korea collection. Some people are denied even this small comfort. I have a friend, a very pretty girl named Margaret Mary who, in spite of the fact that her weight fluctuates wildly (that is to say, she keeps getting fatter) continues to buy chic clothes at fashionable boutiques. Of course she can't wear them. And she tells me that when she opens her closet doors it gives her the sensation of drowning. It's as though all the sins of her past life were swimming before her eyes.

The question is: What do you do with a closet full of unused velvet Capri pants or sequined bikinis? These cannot be dispatched to the deserving poor. Indeed, they don't even make good dusters. They just hang there, a reminder of the folly of human aspirations and the futility of nine-day diets.

How to talk to a baby

Celebrities don't intimidate me. It's babies that intimidate me. Or at least it's with babies that I make such a fool of myself. I'm so afraid I won't make a good impression on them, I'm so afraid they won't be able to place me the next time we meet, that I talk too much—and with the frenzied animation of a nervous guest on the Tonight Show. I also rattle bracelets to get the baby's attention, and wave small objects in the air and burst into snatches of song. This is naturally very boring to the baby, who fastens me with a glance of such unblinking, such crystalline intensity that I know perfectly well what he's thinking. He's thinking "What *is* the matter with that poor soul?"

I find that I have more success when I affect indiffer-

ence, because babies, like some men, seem to like you better if you are unattainable. I remember a time when I marched into Katharine Josephine's room and pretended to be surprised to discover that somebody was occupying the bassinet. "Don't tell me *you're* still here!" I exclaimed. "Listen, kid, do you know what day it is? It's the ninth, you're four months old, and you're not getting any younger, let me tell you. These are your best months and what are you doing with them? Nothing. For your information, babies a lot smaller than you are already out advertising North Star Blankets and you just lie here fluttering your fingers!"

She seemed to hang fascinated on my every word, and then broke out a battery of smiles, oh, a waterfall of smiles—crinkles, wrinkles, dimples, and little gurgling sounds. Naturally, I went to pieces and said the wrong thing. "Oh, goodness!" I said. "You really are the dearest little creature, the sweetest little thing, Mommy's little lamb chop." That did it. All smiles stopped, and it was clear to me our revels now were ended. Immediately she assumed that pained and aloof expression that makes her look like Queen Elizabeth I bidding farewell to the troops. I had to snub her for an entire hour before she'd speak to me again.

It's an interesting fact that babies who won't smile for love or money will smile for vegetables. And the messier the vegetable the more they will smile. A baby with a mouth full of strained spinach is almost guaranteed to smile from ear to ear, while green rivulets ooze down into his neck and all over his wrapper. Now most people make the foolish mistake of trying to scoop the spinach back into the baby's still-open mouth. They also try to reason with the baby: "No, no, honey, don't laugh any more, Mommy's got spinach all over her stockings and—no, oh *no*, not on the rug!"

The best procedure at this moment is to be silent. You are not going to get the baby to see things your way. And anything you do say will merely indicate how completely you have lost your grip on the situation. For instance, to say "Okay, I hope you're satisfied, it's just five minutes since you had a bath and now you're a mess, a complete mess!" will cause you to lose dignity. And since the baby will find that remark pretty hilarious it will cause him to lose more spinach.

Some adults who find themselves uneasy in the silence have discovered that it is helpful to intone, rhythmically, the names of the entire family: "Here's a bite for Grandma, here's a bite for Daddy, here's a bite for Christopher." If the family should be small and the dish of Pablum large, the list can be padded by adding the names of all the delivery men. A friend of mine has worked out a variant of this for her little boy. With the first bite of food she says, "Open up the garage doors, here comes the Chevvy, here comes the Cadillac," and so forth. That child took the game so seriously that eventually he would only eat foreign cars.

But any method is better than the method I used on our first baby. In those days I believed in enthusiasm and the hard sell. I also believed that if a baby missed a single meal it died or something. And I tried to conceal my panic with spurious cheer. "Oooh, yummy, yummy," I would say, sounding like some manic commercial, "Oooh, what have we got *here*? Tasty, tasty Pablum. Oooh, I wish *I* could have some of this delicious Pablum." Then, to indicate that all was on the level, I would actually eat a spoonful or two. Even when I didn't gag, my expression would give the whole show away. In due time that baby found out who was in charge. He was in charge.

Now, light years later, I find I get better results with total candor. I put the cards on the table with the Pablum. "That's right, honey," I say, "it tastes just like library paste. But remember this—it's full of niacin, thiamin, and riboflavins. Furthermore, you really don't have any taste buds yet, so what's the difference? Come on, let's get it right down the hatch!" This seems to work just fine, and you have the satisfaction of knowing that you are building a relationship that is not based on a tissue of lies.

By the way, many people make the false assumption that because a baby can't speak he can't hear. As a result, when confronted with an infant, any infant, they raise their voices and speak very distinctly, as though they were ordering a meal in a foreign language. "Oh, is this the baby?" they ask. (Who else would be sitting in the middle of that playpen—George C. Scott?) "Well, she doesn't look like any of the others, does she?"

A baby will put up with a certain amount of this, but sometimes the remarks get too personal. We once had a visitor who stared at Katharine Josephine (by that time Kitty, and a ripe sixteen months) and, after a minute, said, "Walter, I think she's going to have your nose." Kitty was quite properly irate. She immediately stopped winding her musical egg. And she wouldn't smile. And she wouldn't say "Hi!" on her pink plastic telephone. She wouldn't do anything, and who could blame her?

By contrast, her godfather dropped in that same night. He noticed that she was wearing her Bavarian dress with the white ruffled blouse and all the petticoats, and he said, "Hey, didn't I see you in *The Sound of Music*?" Well, we couldn't shut her up. She let loose a volley of pear-shaped vowel sounds, with a few consonants here and there. And, while I don't pretend to understand her exactly, I'm sure she was explaining that they really *wanted* her for the part and that it was all a matter of conflicting schedules. The point is that little girls of sixteen months appreciate compliments just as much as great big girls of forty.

Another thing: since a conversation between an infant and a grown person is hardly likely to be memorable, most adults don't remember what they have said to the children. But sometimes the children remember. When our Gregory was about two years old, he had the power and the velocity of a torpedo. So the simple business of taking off his clothes and putting on his pajamas turned into a chore roughly equivalent to the landing of a two-hundred-pound marlin. It wasn't just that he wouldn't lie down or sit down or even that he always pulled his arms out of the tops of his pajamas at the precise moment you were sticking his feet into the bottoms of his pajamas. The real problem was that when you tried to put your arms around him in order to snap the various snappers, he shot into the air like a fountain, tumbling over lamps and spilling bottles of baby oil all over the wallpaper.

It wasn't to be expected that I would remain silent during this ordeal. But I honestly didn't know what I had been saying until I listened to Gregory one night after he *had* gone to bed. He was muttering something over and over to himself. What he was muttering was "Oh, my God—your poor *mother!*" We can't have that. I mean I guess we can't have that.

While admitting that adults frequently make unfortunate remarks to babies, it has to be said that babies, too, can make mistakes. Last week Kitty made a real whopper.

Her vocabulary is, of course, limited. But she can pronounce the names of all her brothers as well as the name of the man who comes to fix the dishwasher. Also the name of the nice girl who comes on Friday to clean. "Bessie there," she says with winning clarity. She can also say "Mommy" and "Daddy," of course. The only problem is that sometimes she calls me "Mommy" and sometimes she calls me "Daddy." And there is no excuse for this because my husband and I don't look the least bit alike. Personally, I have never let myself get touchy about the matter because I figured that down the years it would be cleared up. But not everybody is so high-minded. My husband, for instance, reacts to being called "Mommy" by making unworthy remarks like "Okay, wait'll she comes to *me* for an allowance."

As I say, I was philosophical until last Thursday. I went to pick her up after her nap. She smiled the kind of smile that would give you hope even in February. Then she held up her arms and said, very distinctly, "Hi, little fella."

Now, honestly.

As I was saying to a geranium

I had to put a philodendron to death last week, and I still feel terrible about it. Actually, it was a perfectly nice little plant when I bought it two years ago for seventy-five cents. And in the beginning it seemed to thrive on the coffee table, where it put out shiny, fat leaves in a responsible fashion.

But, like so many of us, that plant didn't know when to stop, and it grew and it grew until it spread out all over the table and down the sides. When you picked it up to dust the table, you had to hold the pot in one hand and throw a great train of greenery over your shoulder. Now I would have put up with that. The real problem was that the leaves had become smaller and smaller and limper and limper and had moved so far away from their source that, in effect, what you were looking at was a pot full of dirt with a few brownish-looking legs sticking out of it. I am told that if I had "cut it back" at the proper moment this would never have happened. But I never know when to cut back. When the proper moment comes, we seem to be out to dinner or something.

In any case, it was clear that that plant had to go. But how? Where? I have known terrible people who disposed of unwanted cats by letting them out of the car in a strange neighborhood. But you couldn't do that with a plant and, in any case, in this vicinity there is a fifty-dollar fine for littering. I thought of drowning it, but that seemed impractical, and of course it wouldn't burn. Finally, I gathered it up in my arms and, feeling like a Herod loosed upon the innocents, I walked out into the driveway and dumped it into the trash can. After the deed was done I made myself a stiff drink, but I felt shaky for several hours.

I suppose I did neglect that plant. On the other hand, it would appear that some plants, like some children, require a little neglect. Two years ago a friend sent us a magnificent orange tree that was planted in a handsome Italian ceramic crock. It took two men to deliver it, and they were so patently exhausted by the time they got it from the truck to the door that I told them just to leave it there in the front hallway. As it turned out, that was the perfect place for it—against the bare brick archway. I watered it whenever it crossed my mind and, as the weeks passed, it grew even more beautiful and the tiny oranges turned golden. I would say that I found true

happiness with that orange tree. I never went through the hall without stopping to admire it.

Months later, another friend who is widely consulted as an amateur gardener came to dinner. Roger took one look at my orange tree and recoiled in horror. "Good heavens!" he said. "You can't leave this tree here!" "Why not?" I asked. "Well, for one thing, it's too cold here. And every time that door opens the tree is in a draft. Furthermore, the light's wrong. That's a north light. And *feel* that dirt. It's too dry!"

He couldn't have sounded more accusing if he had discovered one of the children starving and chained to a bedpost. I agreed, naturally, that the tree must be rescued at once. Thereupon three of us hauled it, huffing and puffing, into a safe, sunny spot in the living room.

That tree never had another well day. Almost immediately it developed that clammy look that children get just before they come down with the sniffles. Then the leaves started to curl. Pretty soon you couldn't read in the living room for the plop, plop, plop of oranges as they dropped like ping-pong balls to the floor. We called in our friendly florist for advice. We gave it special plant-food. We gave it more water, less water. Nothing availed. Too late we thought of returning it to the hallway. It had slipped away.

For this reason I pay no attention to Roger on the subject of my tulips. I planted them in the back yard ten years ago and they've been there ever since. According to my friend Roger, this is a sorry state of affairs. Every fall he keeps telling me that those tulips should not be out there in that border, they should be in the house "resting." (Presumably upstairs in the twin beds. And resting from *what?*)

I don't feel that way at all. Next year I don't want to have to hunt all over the house for those tulips. I want to know exactly where they are. And anyway, even if you were going to give them a winter vacation, *when* would you dig them up? Certainly not while they're blooming. And after they've stopped blooming you can't find them.

For the record, I will confess that our tulips are no longer the proud, pristine chalices that once they were. Indeed, they have a faintly tipsy air about them. But they are still bright and cheery and they come back faithfully, which is all I ask of a tulip—or of anybody else, for that matter.

You have no idea what foolish theories some people have about plants. My next-door neighbor believes in an after-life for poinsettias. According to her, when the blossoms have wilted you must pinch them off. Next you place the pot containing the remains in a warm, dark place in the attic, where you water it every five days. Then in May you take it out and plant it in the garden. In September, you dig up the shoots and move them to a sunny window indoors. Eventually, if you have been constant in your ministrations, the plant should bloom again.

Listen, I would do all that for a friend but not for a three-dollar poinsettia. Furthermore, if you kept *all* the poinsettias you get, you wouldn't have room in that attic for the trunks. Actually, what I like best about a big, healthy poinsettia is that it lasts about two and a half weeks, which is enough, and then it goes out when the Christmas ornaments come down. Anything else upsets the natural order of things. For instance, two years ago we received a beautiful white poinsettia, and it bloomed on, not losing a leaf, after all of the red ones were gone. We were charmed when it was still there on St. Valentine's Day. It was even amusing that it survived until Easter. But by July first there was something downright sinister about the whole thing, and people visiting us would say "That *can't* be a poinsettia, can it?" I think they were bracing themselves to find a trimmed Christmas tree in the next room and learn that we were celebrating early because we didn't expect to live until the Feast proper. And when that plant died (a natural death) in August, there was much relief. It boils down to this: if you're going to live to be a hundred and ten, you're going to be in the way.

There was a time when I supposed that I knew, at least in theory, how plants grew. However, it now appears that plants need more than sunlight and water. They need conversation. Librettist Alan Jay Lerner, who had been doing some research on extrasensory perception, explained the matter in the *Times* a while back. "Anybody can make flowers grow by talking to them," he said. "It's a fact. Take two flower pots with the same soil, the same seeds, the same amount of water, and talk to one of the pots. You'll see for yourself."

I don't doubt this for a minute. But it does present certain problems. To begin with, what do you *say* to the pot? Okay, you can start off with something simple like "Hello, Ivy, how's every little thing? What kind of a night did you have?" But it seems to me that after that the conversation would sort of bog down. The truth is, I'm not any good at small-talk. And how could talk get smaller? The next thing: if you were conducting a controlled experiment with two different plants, would you have to keep the plant you weren't speaking to in a separate room? I mean, you wouldn't want it overhearing you. Maybe it would be enough if you simply made yourself clear on the subject. After a brief chat with the ivy, you could say out loud, "As for the fern on the piano, I have *nothing* to say to you."

No, no. It's too complicated. I have enough trouble talking to the children.

The words that come before the music

or

*How Charming, Intelligent Women Drive
Their Husbands Crazy*

I read a lot today about women's rights. Speaking for myself, I have all the rights I can stand. Think of the rights I have, the freedoms I have, that were totally unknown to my grandmother. Did she have a car so she could drive the kids to the Cub Scouts, to the ballet class, to the orthodontist? Was she free to lay asphalt tiles in the bathroom? Did she have the tiles, or the derring-do, or the bathroom? I tell you, one more right and I'll be carted off to Menninger's.

Of course, women still do have their just grievances. But these have had so much publicity that I'm sure they'll be rectified any minute. Shouldn't we give a little consideration, just a little, to the real underdog—the man?

51

Men, too, are downtrodden, but in ways so subtle that their plight never reaches the newspapers or Walter Cronkite. As of this writing, they haven't even begun to organize.

Let me give you a hint of what the ordinary man, the average husband, is subjected to daily, or nightly. As you probably know, one reason why most women have such pleasant relationships with their doctors is that they don't complain to their doctors. They complain to their husbands. The following scene takes place late at night. Peggy and Jim are preparing to go to bed. Peggy is seven months pregnant.

PEGGY I don't know, Jim. Something terribly odd is happening. If I lean over, I get this awful stabbing pain. It seems to start in my rib cage but then it goes right through to the shoulder blades. I don't seem to remember anything like this when I had Billy.

JIM Did you call your doctor?

PEGGY What would I call *him* for?

JIM Because you have this awful stabbing pain that goes—

PEGGY Oh, for heaven's sake. If everybody called him about every least little thing, he'd never get any work done.

JIM Every least little thing! You just got through saying the pain was *stabbing!*

PEGGY Well, that's true. It slices through me just like a carving knife. But I've learned to deal with that. I mean,

usually if I take some baking soda and lie flat on the rug,
it eases up. What really worries me is my fingers.

JIM   Your fingers, what about your fingers?

PEGGY   When I wake up they're so swollen. Honestly,
they're like bananas. This morning I couldn't even pick
up the alarm clock. It dropped right out of my hand. Did
you hear the clunk?

JIM   When do you see your doctor?

PEGGY   On Tuesday. Helen—that's the girl who does my
hair—she says it sounds to her like I'm getting toxic. What
do you think?

JIM   Look. Helen, who does your hair, is not a diagnostician. I am not a diagnostician. Will you for God's sake
check all these things with your *doctor*?

Later, at the doctor's office:

DOCTOR Well, Peggy, I want you to tell me all about yourself. How are you getting along?

PEGGY Oh, fine, Doctor, just fine. But Jim is getting awfully edgy.

If total felicity doesn't obtain at night, things are hardly a great deal better in the morning. During the following conversation Peggy is seated at her dressing table, making general repairs as she stares into the mirror.

PEGGY Oh, I've got such rotten hair.

JIM That's right.

PEGGY What do you mean by that crack?

JIM Nothing, absolutely nothing. Nothing at all. It's just that every day in the world you say you've got rotten hair. I'm just tired of arguing about it.

PEGGY Well, it's true. I have got rotten hair. It looks like grass. Dead grass.

JIM Now, come on, honey—

PEGGY And it *feels* like dead grass. Other women get their hair set and it looks good for a week. Mine looks good for three minutes. And the next morning it looks like I've slept on a bag of potato chips.

JIM Why don't you shave it all off? You'll look just like Senator Fulbright.

PEGGY If you're going to be so damn funny, you should have a larger audience. You should go on the Johnny Carson show.

54

JIM Honey, what do you want me to do? What do you want me to say?

PEGGY I think I should buy a wig.

JIM *Buy* a wig.

PEGGY But a good wig is expensive.

JIM What's a *good* wig?

PEGGY One that doesn't look "wiggy." One that looks so real you don't even notice it.

JIM Get one. By all means, get one.

It is now ten days later, in the living room:

PEGGY How do I look?

JIM Why, you look just fine.

PEGGY Notice anything?

JIM Is that dress new?

PEGGY Of course not, idiot!

JIM Give me a hint.

PEGGY It cost one hundred and twenty-five dollars.

JIM What did?

PEGGY My new wig.

JIM Well, when am I going to see it?

PEGGY If that isn't you! If that isn't typically you! You never notice *anything*.

Jim is going to get himself in deeper before this scene is over, but we shall mercifully draw a veil over it and move to another evening, along about eleven fifteen. Jim has not enjoyed a movie since he saw Spencer Tracy in *Boys Town* but nevertheless he has agreed to take Peggy

57

to the Townside Theatre because she's going to snap if she doesn't get out, out, out of this house. They are now home again.

PEGGY Boy, that was a rotten movie.

JIM I told you it was going to be a rotten movie.

PEGGY You didn't say it would be *that* rotten.

JIM I couldn't say precisely *how* rotten because I hadn't seen it.

PEGGY Then why were you so sure it would be rotten?

JIM Because I have second sight. Also because I read the reviews. And what the hell did you expect from a movie that's advertised as a "porno classic"?

PEGGY I should have stayed home and watched David Frost. I could have cleaned out the oven. We would have saved seven dollars.

(Pause)

You don't say anything.

JIM No, I don't say anything.

PEGGY Really, Jim, I was embarrassed to be seen walking out of that theater. And that *horrible* actor! What's that disease that men have that makes them sexy every living minute?

JIM Satyriasis. And it's not a disease. I've never been able to catch it.

PEGGY There you go! You see a movie like that and you start talking like that. Why would you ever take me to such a filthy thing?

JIM Because, my dear, you insisted. I will quote your exact words. You said, "I don't want to see *Goodbye, Mr.*

58

Chips. I saw *Goodbye, Mr. Chips* when I was seven. I want to see one of those movies everybody's protesting about."

PEGGY Well, I'm never going to Sweden.

JIM I'm sure that's a wise decision.

PEGGY Not only was it dirty, it was just plain dumb. First we have that orgy with all those bare behinds and all those feathers. Then the two men go off and the two women go off. What's that supposed to mean?

JIM A big girl like you should be able to figure that out.

PEGGY Well, I can't.

JIM Good. Then you have been spared something. Now, we both agree it's a rotten movie. Can we stop talking about it?

PEGGY Okay. But just tell me what they were supposed to be doing.

JIM Do yourself a favor, Peggy. Just forget it.

PEGGY Not until you tell me.

JIM Okay, I'll tell you.

(He tells her)

PEGGY You're making that up! I don't believe it for one single minute. You know something? You've got a dirty mind.

One final example. Peggy and Jim are going to spend a week in the Hamptons. Peggy promised to be ready at ten o'clock so that they would miss the heavy traffic on the Expressway. However, she had to write three letters and call her mother long-distance, so it is now two o'clock.

They are in the car, heading for the Throgs Neck Bridge. The vacation has begun.

JIM Okay, what have you forgotten this time?

PEGGY What do you mean *this* time? I didn't forget anything last time.

JIM You mean you've forgotten what you forgot?

PEGGY What are you talking about?

JIM I'm talking about your grasshoppers, or whatever you call those shoes you *walk* in, and how you had to slop around Oldhampton for a whole week in your bedroom slippers.

PEGGY Oh, yes. Well, I've got them.

JIM What about your various pills?

PEGGY I have them.

JIM You're certain you have those yellow ones you take when the water disagrees with you?

PEGGY I have the capsules.

JIM How about that glop you pour on your legs so the mosquitoes will be poisoned?

PEGGY Honestly, you'd think we were going to the North Pole.

JIM There are no mosquitoes at the North Pole.

PEGGY There's a drugstore. We can buy things.

JIM There is one drugstore which is open for twenty-two minutes a day, some days. The last time I had to drive thirty miles to buy one eighty-nine cent bottle of "No-Bite," or whatever they call it.

PEGGY I have it. I have everything. Why do you treat me like the village idiot?

60

JIM I have my own reasons for treating you like the village idiot. Do you have your raincoat and a heavy sweater and a scarf?

PEGGY Yes. Yes. Yes. And I have underwear and slips and stockings and slacks and sneakers and a bathing cap and a shower cap and a sleeping mask and toothpaste and sun-tan lotion and—

JIM Okay. Calm down, calm down.

PEGGY Is the inquisition over?

JIM Yep, all over. Here, will you look at this map and see if you can find out where we pick up Route Sixteen?

PEGGY Oh, honey, we've got to go back.

JIM What's the matter? What happened?

PEGGY I forgot my glasses.

Certain questions pose themselves. Is there any hope for Peggy? No. Is there any hope for Jim? No. In a situation where both parties are absolutely equal because there is no hope for either of them, which party has to go to the wrong movies, provide free medical care, and turn the car around on the highway and drive twenty miles back for a pair of glasses that will eventually turn up in the glove compartment?

I thought you'd guess.

Partying is such sweet sorrow

I always study reports on how the very rich entertain because I know I have a lot to learn. Actually, I could learn something from the way the poor entertain, like, for instance, where do *they* put the playpen when they have people in? But you never read about that.

I note, however and without any glee at all, that the rich make mistakes even as you and I. Just last week the Baroness Guy de Rothschild was confiding her problem to Thelma Sweetinburgh (actual name) in the Sunday *Times*. The Baroness was discussing a party she had given in Ferrières, her weekend château. Now that the ball was over, she had come to one definite conclusion. "Sixteen hundred people are just too many," she said.

See, I would have known that. In our weekend house

(which we also use during the early part of the week) I
have occasionally had as many as twenty-two people and
I can't even keep *them* straight. I was once bidding good
night to a rather quiet visitor and said—I still blush to
think of it—"Oh, you did come, did you?"

But how would you say good night to sixteen hundred
people? I suppose over a public address system. And then,
after the first thousand left, you could sit up and have a
quiet nightcap with the six hundred that remained. That's
always the best part of the evening.

Well, as even the Baroness now realizes, sixteen hundred
people is not a party, it's an emerging new nation.

Another internationally famous hostess, Mrs. Fleur
Cowles, had a close thing recently. It appears that Mrs.
Cowles has an estate about an hour and a half from
London. She also has an apartment in the city of London.

Evidently it is Mrs. Cowles' wont to have the staff of the country house prepare a dinner and bring it in hampers to the apartment in London.

I had always supposed there were difficulties inherent in bringing the mountain to Mohammed, and so it proved. The guests had assembled one Sunday night in Mrs. Cowles' London apartment and were munching canapés when it was discovered that, due to some oversight (an inadequate hamper-check, probably), the main course had been left in the country.

Naturally, the guests couldn't be allowed to drink for the three hours required to fetch the food. By that time they'd have required intravenous feeding. And no butcher shops were open.

Mrs. Cowles paled but did not panic. Nor did she make any kind of general statement, such as "I hope everybody here likes peanut butter." No, she drew a South American Ambassador into a corner and told him all. He had the solution in a trice. One quick call to his staff and everything was arranged. Within the hour the guests were consuming a delicious entrée that had been sent over from the Embassy and no one was the wiser—except, of course, the Ambassador's staff.

Which brings me to my real question. What did the Ambassador *say* when he called home? I try to imagine it. I presume he reached the butler. . . .

"Albert, this is the Ambassador. We are having dinner with Mrs. Cowles. Oh, you knew that. Well, here's the thing. Mrs. Cowles seems to have left the dinner in her other house. What? Yes, that is very bad luck indeed. Now,

I was wondering if you and Cook could fix up thirty-two dinners. Albert, I never joke. Oh, anything, stuffed squab, perhaps some veal scallopini. Now, Albert, that is a very big refrigerator and there surely must be something in it. Albert, I thought the British never cried. Just you put on your thinking-cap and the car will be there in half an hour to pick up the hampers."

You will see that in my anxiety to improve as a hostess I do literally comb the society columns. I must learn how the *in* people entertain. Sometimes this can be very baffling. For instance, during her last visit to New York, Princess Margaret was entertained at dinner by a stage director and his beautiful wife. The menu, as reported in the papers the next day, included "creamed purée of mashed potatoes and chicken on a bed of tarragon."

I want to know more about this. What *is* creamed purée of mashed potatoes? Mashed potatoes? W*atery* mashed potatoes? And as for that chicken on a bed of tarragon, I just don't know. It's been my experience that a pinch, or a sprig, of tarragon goes a long way. Wouldn't a bed be too much? How much *is* a bed? I know it isn't anything like a twin bed—but still. You can't get hold of recipes if they are going to be as vague as that.

Actually, the only reason *I* don't give chic, elegant dinner parties that are the talk of my whole set is that I get faint just thinking about it. In the first place, I don't know who to invite. In theory, I should invite the people who have already entertained us at dinner. In practice, it doesn't work out that way. We live in Larchmont, a small community about twenty miles from New York. Most of our friends live in New York City, and they invite us to dinner calm in the assumption that we will find our way to the great metropolis in less than forty minutes. To a reasonable person it would appear that the distance between New York and Larchmont is approximately the same as the distance between Larchmont and New York. However, when I invite people out here I am left with the feeling that I am inviting them to Ice Station Zebra and that I should offer to provide Sherpa guides for those last tortuous miles through the mountain passes. You understand that Larchmont is on Long Island Sound and flat as can be. The only place a guide will be required is to get them through our garage where, for reasons I couldn't explain under oath, our six children have stored nineteen battered bicycles.

From the time I have invited the first person, and am therefore committed to the affair, I sink into a state of catatonic torpor, rather as though I was waiting to undergo "exploratory" surgery. My ungracious and typical way of extending the invitation is to moan miserably into the telephone, "Oh, my God, Helen, we're having a party, do you want to come?"

I marvel that anybody comes. Other women have told me that at a time like this they become newly and painfully aware that the draperies are fading, the screens are full of holes, and all the slipcovers are frayed in the arms. I notice things like that, too, but I can put them out of my mind because I have learned if you get enough people in the living room you can hardly see the slipcovers. My anxieties lay elsewhere.

To me having a party is something like having a baby. The fact that you got through the last one alive is not somehow sufficiently reassuring now. My husband tries to penetrate my pre-party gloom by asking intelligent questions: "Good heavens, they're all old friends, what are you so worried about?" I'll tell you what I worry about. First, I worry that nobody will come. Nobody at all, and the family will have to eat Chicken Kiev for a month. Then I worry that they *will* come but will simply refuse to talk to one another as they sit like so many birds on a telephone wire. Then if they do come and they *do* chatter, I worry that they won't touch a bite of food because it is undercooked or overcooked or just plain ghastly. After which there is the ultimate worry. Suppose they come, eat, drink, and make merry—and everybody leaves at a quarter after nine.

That actually happened to a woman I know. The poor thing hasn't been right since. Her husband has now sent her to a psychiatrist, even though, as I understand it, it was all his fault because he kept threatening to show movies of Debbie's confirmation.

But I see that I'm gliding past a real crisis area: what to serve. When I was very young I used to serve roast stuffed turkey and baked ham at *every* party. There were two reasons for this. First of all, I like turkey and ham. And secondly, I have (if I may say so) an excellent recipe for turkey dressing.

Down through the years I did notice that none of the people who invited us to dinner ever served turkey and ham. I never criticized them. I just thought they were too lazy to bake a turkey. Certainly I didn't dream I was placing myself in jeopardy socially.

Gradually the truth was borne in on me. In fact, it wasn't all that gradual. A chic friend of mine (you'll know how chic she is when I tell you she makes her own noodles) took me aside one evening and said, "Jean, turkey is traditional at Thanksgiving and Christmas. It is also suitable for sending to policemen who are snowbound. Otherwise—" And she shook her head sadly.

It's really awful to feel embarrassed retroactively. But, dammit, they used to eat that turkey. They even came back for seconds. However, I am easily intimidated. Wishy-washy, really. A twine would lead me. And so now I try to plan a main course that will be a "conversation piece" in spite of the fact that I *know* it's the conversation that should be the conversation piece.

With this in mind I go through all of the recipes I have torn out of magazines during the past six months—a fruit-less enterprise, since the recipes turn out to be "New Tricks with Tuna," "A Wonderful Stew for Weight-Watchers," or "It's February, and it's Shad, Shad, Shad."

Obviously, truly well-adjusted people don't go into this sort of swivet over what they are going to serve as a main course. Last year I was actually invited to one of those parties I spend so much time reading about. This one was so grand that Governor Rockefeller was one of the guests. The host and hostess were perfectly charming, the house was exquisite, the art collection was fabulous, and the dinner was fried pork chops.

I hasten to add that the chops were absolutely succulent and delicious. The Governor ate both of his. And I think everybody there was as relieved as I was that we were not (once again) being served filet of beef, roast of beef, loin of beef, or beef of beef.

The point is that I am not rich enough to serve fried pork chops to company. For that you have to have panache, a certain *élan*, and probably a special kind of pork chop.

As a matter of fact, even fried pork chops aren't all that simple to prepare. I mean, you can't slap them into a pan and just forget about them. An untended pork chop will look like and taste like a wet mitten. Does anybody but me remember when President and Mrs. Roosevelt entertained the King and Queen of England at Hyde Park and served them hot dogs? There, that's real class.

I have all the people coming to dinner next week. Do you suppose I could possibly—? No, no, no, of course not.

I saw Mommy kicking Santa Claus

There's nothing like an old-fashioned Christmas—goodies on the groaning board, halls decked with holly berry, gaily wrapped presents piling up on the window sills, loved ones chiming carols. It can put you flat on your back for a month. For years I spent the whole of January in bed with what was diagnosed as "my brochitis" but was clearly battle fatigue brought on from my days in Macy's and my nights in Bloomingdale's.

It was all my own fault. I had no sense and no system. Only staying power. I was always the last woman on the last down elevator as the store was closing. As a consequence, I was the first one out of the "play" area on Christmas Day. I used to spend the entire afternoon huddled in a chair next to the oven, ostensibly to baste the turkey, actually to put as much distance as possible between me and toys that tooted and growled and beeped and trilled and said "Hey, Doc, wanna carrot?"

It was in this retreat that my husband discovered me one typical Christmas afternoon. He studied my wan and woebegone expression and said, not unsympathetically, "You know, we have two spirits of Christmas around here. We have Santa Claus and then we have anti-Claus—you." And he was right, of course. I had spent all my energy planning and shopping for the Great Day and now that it was here I was, for all practical purposes, absent, a bump on the yule log.

It now seems to me, looking back in anguish, that I hadn't been shopping to buy things, I was shopping to shop. I mean, shop *around*. A person of any intelligence who was looking for a red and black cowboy suit in size eight would buy the first red and black cowboy suit (size eight) that turned up at a reasonable price. Not me. I felt compelled to go to five more stores and check on *their* cowboy suits. Perhaps these might be cheaper or blacker or redder. I could spend an entire afternoon selecting a rattle for a five-month-old infant even though I had already observed that this infant preferred to play with the lids of old cold-cream jars and a tin spoon.

Even so, I was all right years ago when the department stores—in their mercy—used to delay their decorating until after Thanksgiving. Then we had a breathing space, a time to be thankful before it was yet time to be joyful. Now the decorations go up any time after Labor Day, and I suspect they'll be sneaking back to Veterans' Day any minute. You can be wandering down Fifth Avenue on a day of golden Indian summer, thinking your own thoughts, step inside the store to buy nothing more than a pair of nylons, and suddenly find the place a thicket of holly and a downpour of tinsel. When this happens, I panic. I get the same sinking feeling that I experience when the pilot's voice comes over the intercom saying "Fasten your seat belts, we are moving into turbulence." In the plane and in the shop I have the same sensation: *It's all over and I've done nothing.*

I don't know what these merchants have in mind. Maybe they're just trying to be helpful. But I'll tell you what I think. I think they've escalated Christmas.

In the days of my energy, not only did I shop like one demented. I made Christmas decorations *with my own hands.* I, who cannot place eighteen perfect roses in a vase without losing either six roses or the vase, used to experiment with pine cones and lemons. With every florist shop in the neighborhood filled with charming and in-expensive arrangements, I had to paint sticks and glue sequins on them. They looked awful. I will draw a veil over my efforts to create a castle centerpiece from a cardboard box and three thousand gumdrops. For your information, gumdrops will stick to carpets and to sweaters and to cats. They will not stick to cardboard. But I was intrepid.

By Christmas Eve I was so rattled from being intrepid that I couldn't even make a simple decision of policy like: Does Santa bring the tree or does Daddy bring the tree? For years Santa brought the tree, which is ridiculous. It's

75

just one more burden for Santa added on to everything else in that sleigh. It's also one more burden for Daddy since, under these terms, the tree can't be purchased until after dark on Christmas Eve and it can't be trimmed until the small children go to sleep, which could be as late as ten o'clock. The obvious thing, the humane thing, is for Daddy to buy the tree to *welcome* Santa and to *show* Santa where to put the presents. This way it can be trimmed any old time, even by the small children, if you have lots of extra ornaments. But that was a solution which came to me years later.

Another thing that came to me years later was that I ought to buy an axe. Since the trees were pretty well picked over by the time we got out to buy the one that Santa was going to bring, we were invariably stuck with a tall, skinny tree which was four feet higher than the ceiling or a short, fat tree with a trunk too wide for the Christmas-tree holder. Lacking the proper tools, we used to hack at the trees with bread knives and tiny toy saws, a practice which led to wistful exchanges:

"Honey, why don't we buy an axe?"

"We *did* buy an axe."

"Then where is it?"

"We hid it so the children wouldn't find it."

"Where did we hide it?"

"We don't know. The children never found it."

Another thing you need an axe for is to uncrate the toys. Oh, wouldn't it be wonderful if some manufacturer would make a toy as tough, as staunch, as hard to crack open as the carton it comes in! I never did learn any right way to open these seamless, impenetrable fortressess. I do know some wrong ways: jumping up and down on what may or not may be the lid, kicking and clawing with bare fingernails, attacking them with ice skates.

I have often found myself wondering what model household inspired the bard who penned the immortal lines, "And all through the house not a creature was stirring, not even a mouse." We used to stir until six in the morning. Once the tree had been trimmed (late), and the cartons opened (later), we began the real work of the night, which was to put together all the toys that had arrived in separate pieces. It has been explained to me that toys are packaged in shards, to be assembled by the middle-aged and butter-fingered, because this makes it easier for the shippers. It has not been explained to my satisfaction. I am sure that shippers are human. I am also sure that they are, none of them, fathers. If they had to spend hours and hours putting handlebars onto bicycles and fumbling through the wrappings to find the spring marked A that must be attached to the C sprocket of the rail marked YF, they would repent their ways and deliver something that looked like a rocking horse and not like the result of a small street accident.

Anyway, I used to get to bed at six and try to sleep very fast so that I could arise larklike at seven. Alas, I was never larklike. Once up I could do nothing more than subside gently into the softest pile of discarded wrappings, a wreck, gazing glassy-eyed at the frolicking children and moaning in a low voice: "Please save the cards. Don't

77

throw away the cards. You won't know who to *thank* if you throw away the cards."

It's one thing to watch tiny children open their presents. They peck at them delightedly, like young birds discovering worms, completely unselfconscious and really surprised. It's harder, and just a bit heartrending, to watch the older children. They feel obliged to affect surprise. They know 'tis the season to be merry, and they try— oh, so loyally—to measure up. They now perform with the unbelievable bravado of those children in television commercials who seem to get such fun out of brushing their teeth. A twelve-year-old boy will look you not quite straight in the eye and exclaim, "Hey! A racing bike! Boy, I never thought I'd *get* it!" Now, this kid knew all the time he was getting a racing bike because he's been prowling the attic for weeks and found it November 27th. Furthermore, he knows that you know he knew. But the amenities must be preserved. Of course, sometimes he will really be surprised and then he will be marvelously gallant: "Gee, that's swell. Now we have *two* Monopoly games."

Even before all the presents are unwrapped, the battery crisis will have begun:

"Why is he crying?"

"Because his dinosaur won't go any more."

"Why won't it go?"

"Because Col took the battery for his fire engine."

"Col, that fire engine has its own battery."

"No, it doesn't."

"Then use the battery from the Marx-a-Cart."

"That's too big."

"Give him back his battery."

"It seems to be dead now."

Some enterprising youth should go from door to door on Christmas morning peddling batteries. He'd not only make his name and fortune, he'd be first in the hearts of his countrymen. The very worst thing about running out of batteries is that the children are now left free to play with their new games, which would be all right if they would play their new games with each other. But they don't want to play with each other, they want to play with you. Speaking for myself, I don't mind playing any game where there is skill involved. Checkers, for instance. A moderately intelligent adult who is playing checkers with a six-year-old child can usually manage to lose. And in about ten minutes. On the other hand, you can play one of those games with tiny rabbit markers that move forward inch by inch and in which you select cards that tell you—in terrible rhyme—how many hops you may take to the Blueberry Patch. You can play a game like that for one whole hour and then—sweet heaven!—you can *win*. If a child can count, there is absolutely no way to "fix" an Uncle Wiggily game. Soon a sad, defeated voice will be saying to Daddy, "Mommy beat me at Uncle Wiggily." It's degrading. Would you believe that I am the Uncle Wiggily *champ* around here? I am unhinged by all my victories. I am also good at Tinker Toys, probably because I have to pick them up all over the house and it's easier to make something than go find the cylinder they came in.

One thing I am definitely tired of is coloring in coloring books. The reason for this is that children have no sense of quid pro quo when it comes to coloring books. They always want to color the cute little tulips which are so neatly outlined in window boxes, while they insist that *you* color that vast, vacant shape that represents a grizzly bear on a unicycle. It is very boring to make all those long, slashing strokes that never do blend together. And besides, grizzly bears are brown and I hate brown.

Toys can lead to strange new problems and bring about strange new rules ("Do not shoot arrows out of the bedroom window, Do not try out your sled on the stairs, and Yes, I *know* the stair-carpeting won't hurt the runners"). We ran into a really iffy situation two years ago

Whitney
Darrow, Jr.

when Gregory was six. He had received a small, battery-propelled car (*with* batteries, I don't know how it happened) which he drove all day long without respect for life, limb, shin or table leg. I must explain that I am one of those mothers who prefaces most directives with the phrase "I've told you a hundred times (not to leave Coke bottles under the bed, not to crack walnuts with the steam-iron, etc. etc."). On that particular Christmas night we were all finally assembled at the dining-room table and I was busy burning my fingers passing the sweet potatoes when Gregory suddenly got up, left the table solemnly, put on his crash helmet, stepped into his car and sailed out of the room at the majestic speed of three miles an hour. When I recovered from my astonishment, I called after him, "Where on earth are you going?" His tone was quite matter-of-fact. "I'm going to the bathroom," he replied. "Gregory," I began automatically, "I've told you one hundred times—" and then I stopped, noticing the expression on my husband's face, which had suddenly become deeply and genuinely contemplative. At last his brow cleared and he spoke. "I don't *think* you've ever told him he can't go to the bathroom in his Marx-a-Cart," he said.

I suppose I would have gone the rest of my life as the Mad Shopper and January Dropout if it hadn't been for a small accident. What happened was that, four years ago, just as I was getting ready to make my first field trip to 34th Street, I slipped on a crayon and sprained my ankle. A week later the ankle was two ankles, though on the same foot. Clearly I couldn't get to Bloomingdale's when I was having trouble getting to the sink. I sulked like a ball player who's been benched in the last inning, I inveighed against the powers that be, I cursed all crayons. I knew how important executives solve the problem; but you can't mail a seven-year-old child a card telling him that a donation has been sent in his name to UNICEF. And my husband's suggestion that *he* do the shopping I ruled out entirely. I still remember the time he bought an electric letter opener for a five-year-old boy on his birthday. When I made the obvious remark, "But that kid doesn't get any mail," he cheerfully said, "That's all right, he can open ours." This might have worked out all right if this boy had confined himself to opening letters that were coming *in*.

Eventually, but only eventually, I came to my senses. Then I used my head, I used the store catalogues, I used the telephone. Did you know that the eight red Santa Mugs (@ 4.98) that you order on the telephone are exactly the same Santa Mugs that you go from the third floor to the seventh floor to the fifth floor to find? It doesn't make any sense, but I once truly believed that if I had to stand in line for twenty minutes to have a package gift-wrapped it actually gave the recipient more pleasure.

Anyway, that's all behind me now. The only thing I insist on seeing with my own eyes, touching with my own hands, is batteries. In the hardware store I pick over—and perhaps bruise—batteries the way some women handle tomatoes. Locally, I am known as the Battery Lady. But, you see, I have time for such things nowadays. I even have time to listen to the children while *they* trim the tree. Last Christmas I heard Gregory explain to his brothers that he was leaving two doughnuts for Santa on the very lowest branch of the tree because Santa must be a short person. If he was small enough to fit in the chimney he couldn't be big enough to reach a high doughnut.

Let me tell you how hale I was all day last Christmas, and how I entered into the spirit of everything. I was playing *Rollo Revels and Romps Away*, the only composition I know, on Kitty's toy piano when I received a request: "Hey, Mom, would you stop playing that thing for one minute so I can hear what this rabbit says?"

We had a lovely Christmas, thank you, and I hope you had the same.

I don't want to see the uncut
version of *anything*

Reflections of a Part-Time Playwright

Recently I was heard to murmur against the endless frustrations connected with getting a play produced. I mean I was exploding in all directions and pounding on the table with the handle of a broom. My husband finally quieted me by saying, "How can you complain so much—do you know that Euripides was *exiled?*" Actually, I didn't. But now that I know, it makes all the difference. In the future when shadows gather and vexations mount, I shall take solace from the fact that, in any event, I was never exiled.

But I don't mean to talk about playwriting. My experience as a playwright is so limited that I think it would be hasty for me to theorize about it. On the other hand, because of my husband's sorry occupation, my experience as a member of the audience is enormous. It occurs to me that in the last eighteen years I have become the most experienced audience in America.

We are agreed that a critic is not, and never will be, a member of the audience. Not only is he paid to attend, he is paid to listen; and this sobering circumstance colors his whole attitude toward the material on stage. The critic says: This is an extremely bad play—why is that? The audience says: This is an extremely bad play—why was I born? There is a real difference.

Anyway, on those melancholy opening nights when one sees that the jig is up and the closing notice soon will be, I make little notes to myself. I list some of them here in the wistful hope that somewhere there is a beginning playwright who will believe that my prejudices are shared by some other people. I think they are. I think I am pretty close to being the square root of the *ordinary* audience. I notice that I perk up when other people perk up. I slump when they slump. And I most certainly do not keep my head when all about me are losing theirs. I think paradise will be regained on 44th Street when young playwrights understand that they must try not to write plays that will cause nice, ordinary people from Riverdale to wish they were dead.

Little Notes to Myself:

I believe that plays that are successful are almost invariably more entertaining than plays that fail. This will come as a revolutionary idea only to those who have spent their lives avoiding beautiful girls because they are rumored to be dumb.

It is perfectly all right with me when a character in an

Whitney Darrow, Jr.

avant-garde play points to a realistic iron bed and says, "That is a piano." It is still all right with me when another character sits down in front of the bed and plays *The Blue Danube Waltz* on the mattress. But thereafter I expect that nobody will lie down on the piano.

I think that if there are only three characters in a play, one of them ought to be a girl.

I do not wish to see musical comedies performed entirely on bleachers in which the leading man wears clown-white make-up (the only man in the world who can put on clown-white make-up and be Marcel Marceau is Marcel Marceau).

It strikes me as less than hilarious when an actor, impersonating a foreigner, is required to struggle with our quaint American colloquialisms. ("How ees eet you put it? I shovel you. Ah, no. I deeg you.")

I do not like to hear the most explicit four-letter words spoken from the stage because I number among my acquaintance persons of such candor and quick temper that, for me, the thrill is gone.

I have noticed that in plays where the characters on stage laugh a great deal, the people out front laugh very little. This is notoriously true of productions of Shakespeare's comedies. "Well, sirrah," says one buffoon, "he did go heigh-ho upon a bird-bolt." This gem is followed by such guffaws and general merriment as would leave Olsen and Johnson wondering how they failed.

It may have been bearable the first time it was done, but it is no longer bearable to see a comedy in which the ingenue yap yap yaps the whole first act long about the burdens of her virginity.

Also—speaking of the same kind of play—the heroine always does look as cute as all get out when, for reasons of the plot, she has to wear the hero's bathrobe. On the other hand (and this is happening more and more), when the hero is required to wear her brunch coat, he looks just plain terrible.

I have noticed that an entertainment that opens or closes with the setting up or dismantling of a circus tent always gets good notices. I don't know what to make of this.

I have seen plays performed on steps in front of a cyclorama that I enjoyed—but not many.

I am wary of plays in which God or the devil appear as characters. We will waive any discussion of theology and I don't mean to be irreverent when I say that, for all practical purposes in the theater, God is a lousy part. (A play I really loved, *The Tenth Man*, had to do with a girl who was being exorcised of the devil, but it may be relevant to note that we never saw the devil.)

I don't want to see productions that run four and one-half hours. (I don't want to see the "uncut version" of *anything*.) In a recent production of *King Lear*, the first act ran for two and one-half hours. By that time I considered that I had given up smoking, and I spent the entire intermission wondering if I should begin again. And I was once more made aware—during that interminable first act —that the most serious materials eventually seem comic if they are allowed to go on too long. For instance, during the protracted scene in which Lear (now mad) is talking to poor, blinded Gloucester, all I could think was: first they put his eyes out, now they're going to talk his ears off.

One thing, though. Whatever their losses on other fronts, actors have got to keep their teeth in. I would have thought this went without saying until I saw two plays by Joe Orton. In one a slatternly landlady, who was competing with her brother for the affections of a male lodger, lost her dentures under the sofa. In another, a young man plundered the corpse of his recently dead mother, removing her false teeth so that he could use them as castanets. If this sounds funny, I'm not telling it right.

When *The Little Foxes* was revived recently, there were those who said it was too well constructed. To me, that's like saying a Pan Am pilot is too conscientious. What I like about Lillian Hellman's play is that you couldn't play the second act first. I know all about improvisation and the free-form that mirrors the chaos of our time, but I do like to feel that the playwright has done *some* work before I got there.

I dislike seeing actors perform in the nude. Not that, at my age, I am shocked, but I become exceedingly uncomfortable as the naked performers begin to perspire under the hot lights and develop a tendency to stick to the furniture, or, worse, to each other. In the aura of silliness which prevails on such occasions, I find myself distracted from the plot (which seems merely to be against the audience) into practical considerations. Do they still call them dressing rooms? If an actor develops a boil in an unsuitable area, is a Band-aid used, or the understudy? Is it possible to say to an actor, "I saw you in *Oh, Calcutta*," without laughing?

At plays like *A Man for All Seasons*, *The Matchmaker*, *The Lady's Not for Burning*, *A Streetcar Named Desire*, *The Odd Couple*, *The Great White Hope*, *Summer and Smoke*, and *The Front Page*, I don't make any notes at all. I just sit there and bask and bask and bask and then, when the glow begins to wear off, I go back again.

Marriage: unsafe at any speed

I know what I wish Ralph Nader would investigate next. Marriage. It's not safe, it's not safe at all.

Do you realize that every day the unwary and the unready leap into an arrangement that has no guarantee, no warranty, no money back? Even with the present divorce rate most people still marry with the conviction that they will remain together until death do them part. And, in this enlightened era, that could be one hell of a long time. During the Middle Ages, when whole villages expired early because of the prevalence of plague and the misuse of leeches, this was not such an awesome prospect. But nowadays people who marry in their early twenties have every reason to believe they'll still be kicking in their seventies. In other words, that marriage could last fifty years. What else in the world lasts fifty years—washers, cars, radios, governments?

Think of the innocents who make this staggering commitment for reasons no more coherent than that they feel icy fingers up and down their spine and, what is more curious, hear music when there's no one there. It is not enough to point out that the icy-fingers-down-the-spine stage of marriage is of limited duration. And that those husbands (married over two years) who look for that same old witchcraft when your lips meet mine will be told "Not now, for God's sake, can't you see I'm making dinner?" Actually, it's probably a mercy that these first, fine fevers of romance do abate. I, for one, would not care to go fifty years hearing music when there's no one there. You could get the reputation of being a little bit dotty.

But let's get beyond these rather elementary matters. Have you faced up to the fact that it is harder to get a driver's license than a marriage license? In most states, prospective drivers have to take an eye test, a written test, and a road test. Now surely it would be helpful if persons about to be married were required to undergo an eye test. They should have to prove to some qualified official that they really did see what they saw in each other.

It would be harder, I know, to arrange a road test for marriage which would duplicate the actual traffic conditions. But it could be done. An engaged couple could be asked to live for one week in a third-floor walk-up apartment with four children under ten (two of whom have

colds), a sink that was stopped up, and a puppy that wasn't housebroken. This would prove an eye-opener to the young couple. It would also provide a week's vacation for the real parents of the four kiddies which would, of course, be good for *their* marriage.

Lastly, there absolutely should be a written test. Not only do we want to lower the divorce rate, we want to eliminate the sorry spectacle of married couples who sit in public restaurants for two hours without uttering eleven words between them and then go outside and hiss at each other in the parking lot.

I know that psychiatrists say that the chief causes of trouble in marriage are money, sex, and in-laws. But it has been my observation that it isn't what people *do* in these major areas that's so important, it's what they *say*. (Do you know that there are no recorded instances of divorce among deaf-mutes?) Let me give you an example. My friend Helen had her mother from Arizona visiting for three weeks. Helen's husband Ralph could not have been more saintly. He met Mother at La Guardia. He took her to Radio City Music Hall. He played gin rummy with her. He watched the Lawrence Welk Show. Twice he took her to a restaurant where the only thing served as salad was a sliced pineapple filled with tinted cottage cheese. He allowed her to talk to him all the time he was trying to read the morning *Times*. He was, as I say, saintly.

Then he blew it. Two days after the old lady went back to Arizona he turned to his wife and said, "Helen, I wish you'd lay off that fudge, you're going to be fat and waddle just like your mother."

Helen says she is never going to speak to him again, though of course she will—in time. Ralph, however, is going to have a rough twenty-four hours, at least. And it all could have been avoided. If the specter of Helen turning into Mother really unnerved Ralph, he might have said, "Honey, why don't we both go on a diet and buy some new clothes?" There is a right way to put things and a wrong way. Alas, most people rush like lemmings to make the very remark that is bound to lead to dropped forks, slammed doors, and a Bad Day at Black Rock.

Here is where a written test would help. Just as potential drivers go on record indicating that they are aware that one never parks in front of a fire hydrant, the about-to-be-married ought to show that they are aware that one never asks, "How did you ever get out of high school without learning to add?" or "Is this the same lamb we had three nights ago?"

Now I don't know every wrong statement that can be made in a marriage (my husband would dispute this), but I know some of them. And I have made up my own little multiple-choice test to weed out the unmarriageable.

Since it is barely out of the blueprint stage, I am making things easier by placing the one correct answer *last* in every case. This way you can't cheat by looking up the answers on another page.

FOR MEN

What is the proper answer when the little woman asks the following questions:

How is the roast beef?
  (a) Roast beef? I thought it was potroast.
  (b) Honey, do we have any ketchup?
  (c) Great.
My best friend from college is coming for a couple of days. Is that all right?
  (a) Okay, but don't expect me to steer her through the Guggenheim again.
  (b) Do you mean Grace who twitters like a parakeet and leaves squashed Kleenex all over the house because of her sinus condition?

(c) Of all your friends, Honey, I think Grace is the one most like you.

Can you tell I've lost weight?
  (a) Not really. I'd say you'd have to lose another ten pounds before it begins to show.
  (b) If you say so.
  (c) Wow.

I suppose you wish I was as good a cook as Emmy?
  (a) Or even half as good.
  (b) I'm sure you could cook as well as Emily if you were willing to put the same amount of time into it.
  (c) Oh, I'd get pretty sick of all that rich food day after day. And they say Bill's getting a liver condition.

Do you love me as much as the day we were married?
  (a) Yeah, yeah, yeah, I love you as much as the day we were married.
  (b) Oh, God, not again.
  (c) If you have to ask that question, Honey, it must be my fault. I mustn't be showing all the love I really feel.

Will you lower that damn ballgame?
  (a) If I lower that ballgame, all I'll hear is you screaming at the kids.
  (b) When *you're* listening to Ol' Dave and Ol' Chet, I can hear it as I step off the New Haven.
  (c) Oh, is it bothering you? Why don't I go up to the bedroom and watch it on the portable? You'll be coming up, won't you?

Would you say that I have been a help to you in your work?

(a) Honey, don't make dumb jokes.

(b) Undoubtedly, undoubtedly. If I didn't have you and the kids I'd be a beachcomber today. And very happy.

(c) Honey! Could I ever have got to teach third grade without you right here beside me?

You never talk to me.

(a) I don't talk to you because the only topics in the world that interest you are Billy's rotten report card, your rotten dishwasher, and that rotten milkman who keeps tracking up your linoleum.

(b) Of course I talk to you. What am I doing now, pantomime?

(c) And here I was, sitting here and thinking how beautiful you are and how lucky I am and how peaceful it was.

FOR WOMEN

What is the proper answer when hubby makes the following observations:

What happens to all my clean handkerchiefs?

(a) I eat them.

(b) You don't have clean handkerchiefs because you don't put them to the wash. You leave them all scrunched up in your slacks which are on the floor of the closet.

(c) Here's a clean one of mine. We'll fold it so the lace doesn't show.

Hey, Abe's new wife is attractive as hell, don't you think?
   (a) Everybody's new wife is attractive. Your problem is that you're stuck with your old one.
   (b) Yes, but I think she might do something about that little mustache.
   (c) I think *all* Abe's new wives are attractive.

When you write a check, will you for God's sake, please, please, write down the amount somewhere, anywhere?
   (a) Why do you carry on like a madman? Nothing ever ever happens, the checks never bounce.
   (b) Okay, you're Paul Getty, *you* make out the checks.
   (c) Yes.

Ye gods, does that kid have to eat that way?
   (a) No, I coach him to eat that way because I know it drives you absolutely crazy.
   (b) That kid just also happens to be your kid, and any time you want to give him your famous lecture on table manners, I'll be rooting for you all the way.
   (c) Darling, I *want* to reprimand him but he's so exactly like you I just melt.

Oh, Lord, you're crying again. What is it this time?
   (a) I spent three hours stuffing the veal and you never even said it was good. I had my hair done and you didn't notice. It rained all day and the kids were like maniacs. And after I sewed all the buttons back on Brucie's sweater he lost it in the park. And you never, never, never offer to do anything to help me.

(b) Because I want to marry Aristotle Onassis and live on the island of Scorpia and have a hundred servants and my own airline.

(c) Oh, because I'm silly and I don't count my blessings. Come on, give me a little squeeze and take out the garbage and I'll be through here in no time.

There. Of course I don't mean to suggest that this test is either foolproof or definitive. I mean only to be the first pebble in the avalanche that must surely come. But perhaps I should add just one final cautionary note. Those persons who found themselves anticipating the correct answer *in each instance* are probably so perfect that they would drive any other human being bonkers. I suggest that they remain single.

The Children's Hour after hour
after hour

There is this to be said about little children. They keep
you feeling old.

Naturally, they don't mean to do this. And when a four-
year-old boy presents you with a bouquet that he has picked
himself from your neighbor's prize tulip bed, he has the
best intentions in the world. When this first happens to a
young mother—say, in her early twenties—she can usually
keep her head even if all the tulips have lost theirs. After
all, it *was* rather sweet of Billy, and surely an abject letter
of apology and two dozen roses will square things with
Mrs. Hayden.

If, however, nineteen years later this same woman re-
ceives the same offering of tulips from another four-year-
old boy, brother of the first, she is very likely to snap ("Oh,

good Lord, we're just going to have to move away from here, that's all!"). In the intervening years this woman has lost muscle-tone and confidence. In fact she has lost everything but weight.

The problem of the large or medium large family is that the parents keep growing older and changing, while the children stay the same. One after the other they get the same knots in their shoelaces, the same ink on the sheets, the same pennies in their ears. They lose the same book-bag, they get holes in the same sweaters (sometimes they *are* the same sweaters), and one and all they keep dinner from being a gracious occasion. Let me explain. Our oldest, who is twenty-one, no longer spills milk at the dinner table. (I'm not bragging, I'm just stating a fact.) But of course his baby sister still does. And all the others in between did. Now I do not cry about the spilt milk. I don't even mind cleaning it up. That's why we have plastic table mats. What I do mind (Doctor, I just feel old and tired) is that every night for almost twenty years I have felt obliged to make the banal but stunningly prophetic remark, "Don't leave that glass there, you're going to knock it over with your elbow." But what else can you do? You've got to prepare for the fact that someday one of those kids may be invited out to dinner, and they can't be sloshing milk all over Westchester County.

I'm sick of talking about milk. When do we get to the great topics, like art, music, McLuhan? And what about people like the Kennedys, who, they say, had such brilliant conversation at the dinner table, even when the children were young? How? Didn't those kids get any milk?

Whitney Darrow Jr.

There are those who distinguish between bright children and slow children, between extroverts and introverts. From my point of view—twenty years after—there are only two kinds of children. There are picky eaters. And then there are the stuffers.

The picky eater holds his fork limply, resting his cheek on his left fist and staring at the best-dinner-in-the-world with such evident loathing that all appetites vanish. Now I know that pediatrician Dr. Lendon Smith says "If the child can get up and walk around, he's eating enough," and if I'd ever been able to believe this, my whole life would have been different. But, due to my conviction that one spoonful of mashed potatoes and three cookies does not constitute a balanced diet, I have gone right on making idiotic and demonstrably unworkable rules like: "You're not going to leave this table until you eat every bite of that dinner. Not if it takes all night." I've done this year after year until I don't have to think any more. I'm a pre-recorded announcement. Once, after a prolonged stretch with a particularly picky eater, I was invited to a dinner party. I am told that I caused some astonishment when I remarked, rather crisply, to the gentleman on my right, "Why you haven't touched one thing on that plate but your chicken!"

As for the stuffers, there are two varieties. The first, and quite harmless, sort is the great bottomless pit who can consume more food in a day than one person can carry home from the supermarket—while still remaining lean and sinewy (and bottomless). The true or troublesome stuffer, on the other hand, suffers from a low metabolism and a poor memory, both of which cause him to gain weight. He doesn't seem to realize that the eight square meals he eats a day play some part in his ever-increasing amplitude. To hear him tell it, he was betrayed by a Chiclet. Actually, the effort of consuming three helpings of a turkey dinner mysteriously causes this child to work up an appetite. Before the dinner dishes are yet washed he will require a peanut-butter and jelly sandwich. And if he is not hounded into total alienation by terrorist tactics, such as having his pockets checked for extra brownies and his bureau drawer checked for Cokes (and, would you believe it, chocolate Metrecal), he will presently assume those odd contours that suggest someone removed a cork from his big toe and blew him up. True unhappiness comes when you have a picker and a stuffer at the same dinner table, so that you wind up saying, "Won't you have a little more gravy—no, no, no, not *you!*"

By this time wouldn't you think I could stop sounding like a top sergeant and become the gracious person I am? After all, the whole theory of the well-spaced family is that sooner or later there will be older siblings around to take over some of these chores, like demonstrating the fashionable use of the fork and getting knots out of shoelaces. (Where knots are concerned, my right hand has lost its cunning.) The dream goes something like this. You've been in hand-to-hand combat with a rambunctious two-year-old (and a two-year-old who is not rambunctious is coming down with something) for an entire afternoon. You have removed him from high places, you have taken foreign objects out of his mouth, you have kept him away from

the stove and electrical outlets, you have answered nine hundred and seventy-three questions dishonestly. You are not yourself any longer. Enter his cheerful older brother, the Peace Corps. He says, "Hey, Mom, want me to take this kid for a walk?" It is a moment of magic which makes everything seem worthwhile. I know because it has happened to me as many as three times in twenty years.

If I've grown too old to dream, it's not because the bigger boys are less agreeable. They're just less present. It has been my observation that as soon as a boy has become housebroken and a pleasure to have about, he is no longer about. He's in school all the time. I consider a boy housebroken, by the way, when you can watch him going out the back door into fourteen inches of snow without feeling you ought to say, "Be sure and wear your rubbers." Another sign of maturity in a child is when he no longer asks questions like where is his Batman cape while you are in the middle of a long-distance call ("Stop pestering me. No, Mother, you're not pestering me. I'm talking to Gregory").

Clearly other women have coped better than I can. All the time I find myself ruminating about Longfellow's "The Children's Hour." If I grasp this poem correctly, Longfellow didn't lay eyes on those kids until sometime "between the dark and the daylight when the light is beginning to lower." I take that to be about five-thirty (depending on the time of year). Wasn't that Mrs. Longfellow a marvel to keep those children out of his hair all day long? Remember, he worked at home. I can see it may have been easy enough with Grave Alice. But what about that Laughing Allegra? Can't you just hear her? I'd have been out in that den saying, "Henry Wadsworth, *you* watch Laughing Allegra for an hour!"

Why is it so hard to say *nice* things to children? We're being told all the time that little children need love. All psychiatrists understand this. I think most parents understand it. But there is a whole group that seems to have been left in the dark on this matter. Children. Surely if those kids knew they needed love, they'd be more lovable.

Let's get this thing down to strict logic. Obviously the psychiatrists aren't trying to tell us to love children when they're being adorable. Heaven knows that's easy enough. Even your true Monster Mother (who never made cookies in her life) is tempted to give hugs to a nice little boy who is drying the silver. And when a three-year-old girl looks in the mirror and says, "I'm going to be tall and pretty—just like Mommy," Mommy does not require professional guidance in order to feel loving. Even the psychiatrists, mired as they are in terminology, know this.

So they must mean something else. Apparently they mean that you should love children when they are driving you absolutely out of your mind. But I really don't know how practical that would be. Imagine this scene. Nine-year-old Billy comes home from school. You say to him: "Billy, your teacher called. She said you were late for school again. She also said you didn't bring in your homework any day this week, and that you deliberately spilled water paint on Mary Dee's jacket. Furthermore, she said that you constantly disrupted the entire class with your foolish antics. I love you, Billy."

I think Billy would definitely be rattled. He may be only nine but he's heard a little something about mental illness. I think he would feel better oriented (if that's the word, and it is) if he heard you say what he expects you to say, which is "Just wait until your father hears about this. Just you wait."

It is a mark of really mature, really experienced parents that they are very repetitious. Having learned, down through the years, that small children must be told everything a number of times, they try to cut corners by saying things twice in the first place. For example: "Wash your hands. Did you hear me, I said wash your hands. And with soap. Got that? *With soap.*" The alternative is to wait fifteen minutes and then say, "Look at those hands. Just look at those hands. Do you mean to tell me you think those hands are washed?" Personally, I talk like this all the time, and I hear myself. Hear myself? I hate myself. I sound dithering if not deranged. But that's how you get with a well-spaced family.

The ideal thing, the perfect solution, would be to have sextuplets when you were in your early twenties. Then, when the children were two years old, *all* of them would untie their shoelaces and remove their shoes. It would be quite a pile of shoes, but once that phase was over it would be over. Likewise when the six of them were spilling milk it would be pretty damp around the house for a while— but not forever. I imagine it would be pretty rough the year *all* of them were telling you riddles. But remember. You'd be young and willing to learn which state was high in the middle and round on each end (Ohio, of course, it couldn't be New York). The point is, you wouldn't find yourself at forty still shouting, "Don't run, please don't run! *Not* with that lollipop in your mouth."

Confessions of a sea-lubber

It's strange the number of people who take planes when they might take a ship. I don't understand it. The plane trip is so much longer.

Surely you must have noticed that a whole year goes by between that moment when you fasten the seat belt and the time when the stewardess wheels out that first highball. I've noticed, and I'm not even a serious drinker. But if there are no atheists in foxholes, there are no abstainers aloft. I've seen the most proper people lapping up that third Scotch as though they thought they'd never see another—which is what they thought.

A second reason I always drink on an airplane is out of consideration for the person sitting next to me. Cold sober, I am likely to look out the window. Inadvertently, I mean.

I would never do it deliberately. I'm not sure that I know how things are *supposed* to look when viewed through the window of an airplane, but they never look exactly right to me. And so I clutch the arm of a perfect stranger and ask idiotic questions like, "Good God, is that wing *bending?*"

It always is a stranger sitting next to me because my husband insists upon separate planes. As I understand it, his plan is to crash alone and leave me to bring up all these crazy kids. Or maybe it's simpler than that. Maybe he just doesn't want me to ask *him* all those questions: "What is that scrunching sound?" or "That sign that says the seat cushion may be used for flotation—does that mean what I think it means?" Are they crazy? Where would you float in Washington, D.C.?

Now, while a forty-minute shuttle flight from New York to Washington, D.C., can seem as long as a trip to Jupiter, an eight-day sea voyage to Naples is as fleeting as love's young dream. There are those who mourn the passing of the white sperm whale; I grow melancholy as I watch the passing of the great ocean liners. Not that I am indifferent to the whale situation. I consider myself in the forefront of those who brood about the day-to-day problems of those surviving whales. It's just that I myself have never seen a white sperm whale, so their predicament is not entirely real to me. (I never even saw the movie of *Moby Dick*, though I understand that the Moby was poor, very poor, not even as spirited as Gregory Peck.) But I have seen the old *Queen Elizabeth* and the *Queen Mary* and the *United States*, and when I consider that these liners are gone, gone, gone,

I want to sob or riot or write to my Congressman. (God bless the Italians who keep these big, beautiful ships going to and fro, with spaghetti flowing at lunch *and* dinner.)

Being on a ship is something like being pregnant. You can sit there and do absolutely nothing but stare at the water and have the nicest sense that you are accomplishing something. I mean, you're getting there.

Being on a ship is also really nicer than being in a luxury hotel in a foreign country. You have all the comfort and all the fattening food without being nagged by the feeling that somehow you ought to be out broadening your cultural horizons. For instance, you don't have to think about getting up at dawn, hiring a car, and driving fifty miles into the mountains to see a rare old tapestry in a quaint old chapel.

By the way, those who cannot be deterred from their pursuit of out-of-the-way art objects should be warned that they will undoubtedly find that chapel closed because it happens to be Monday (or Tuesday or Friday or Sunday) or because the chapel is being repaired or because the Vienna Boys' Choir is recording within. The custodian will explain, in the language of the country and with the charm of custodians the world over, "Don't blame me, lady, I don't make the rules, I just work here." Personally, I wouldn't go to see the Pacific Ocean without checking with three responsible people to find out whether or not the Ocean is open on weekends.

Everything on shipboard seems better than life in real life—even the movies. It's not that the movies are better; actually, they're worse. But, for one thing, they're free and you're free. I mean, you can leave and go back to your cabin without having an argument with your husband. ("Oh, come on, be a sport, it's bound to pick up in the last reel.") My husband once got me to sit all the way through *The Fox* (a film about lesbians) because he was curious to see what happened to the fox (who was, I must say, a splendid animal, loaded with talent, a regular Rinty, and probably—I feel certain—sexually impeccable). In any case, being free to leave somehow keeps you sitting there. I know a neurosurgeon who walked out of *The Graduate* at the Sutton Theatre and sat all through *Swingers in Paradise* on the *Michelangelo*.

And people on shipboard are so nice and approachable. At a cocktail party in town, the stranger sitting next to you on the love-seat (in these circumstances shouldn't it be called the like-seat?) will meditate for five minutes before he finally asks, "Well, what do you think of this weather we're having?" Your fellow passengers at sea never ask you such trivial, boring questions. Invariably they sweep to the larger issues and the heart of the matter, and ask "How much do you plan to tip your cabin steward?" (Incidentally, the only conceivable virtue in undertipping is that you will be thought a seasoned traveler and/or rich.)

Speaking of cabin stewards, I still remember my horror on my first crossing (several years back) when I returned to my cabin after a moonlight stroll on deck to discover that the steward had found my ghastly pink seersucker pajamas and had lovingly spread them on the bunk. I wear seersucker pajamas because I like them, and I like them best when they are soft and old and the nap has worn off.

But, as a result of this chastening experience, I always bring along a couple of satin nightgowns which I strew casually about the cabin so that the steward can take some pride in his work. This may seem extravagant, but since I never wear them, they'll never wear out. And unless we actually sink, the steward will never find my seersuckers because I hide them under the life preserver in the closet.

Most people embarking on an ocean voyage bring along a book they've intended to read forever, like *Martin Chuzzlewit* or *The Education of Henry Adams*. I don't find this necessary because (a) I never intend to read *The Education of Henry Adams*, and (b) I find so many interesting things to read right there in the cabin. First, there is this little booklet full of tantalizing information about the ship. You will learn that the keel was laid in Genoa in 1962 (which, I am sure, was a vintage year for keels). In addition, I find it reassuring to learn that the ship is equipped with "Denny-Brown stabilizers with four automatic fins." That sounds about right to me. Six would probably be too many. And, while I don't happen to know anything about the Denny-Brown people, I'm sure they're the best. There is, however, one instruction that always disturbs me. It reads: "Anyone seeing a man falling overboard should shout MAN OVERBOARD STARBOARD or PORT SIDE (Starboard or Port is referred to the right or left of a man facing forward to the bow). Whosoever should hear the call should repeat it loudly and attempt to pass it to the Bridge."

I can't figure that out right this minute, when I have all the time in the world. In an emergency, heavens knows what I'd say. I mean, I know the difference between right and left, but I don't always know where the bow is. As a result, I simply never go on deck unless I am sure that there are a number of responsible people about. I can always put in time in my cabin studying my bilingual dictionary, especially the section marked "Phrases Most Often Used." Others have observed that the authors of these dictionaries do not seem to have a firm grasp of colloquial English. I want to say I am more struck by the fact that they can't seem to get through a page without foreseeing disaster. An air of doom prevails. After intense study, and only a little Dramamine, I am now able to say in flawless Italian, "Conductor, I have experienced misfortunes with my luggage," "Quick, summon a physician, my husband appears to ail," and (my favorite) "Mistress, this plumbing is imperfect and I am unable to bathe."

Another bonus for readers is the Program for the Day, which is slipped under the door each morning. This not only gives you the times of the meals and the titles of the movies but goes on to reveal the wealth of other goodies that await you. "Eleven-thirty: Organ Recital in the Bamboo Lounge. Tunes from Yesteryear." (Okay, but think about it: it's better than tunes from *this* year.) "Three-thirty: Complimentary Dance Lesson on the Main Deck with Florio and Janet, weather permitting." I happen to feel that this "weather permitting" merely injects an empty note of pessimism, but I suppose you can't have people frugging right over the rails.

The best thing of all, though, is the ship's daily newspaper. This is the absolutely ideal publication. It's as peaceful as a Zen garden. No screaming headlines to ruin your breakfast and make you wonder if you shouldn't take the younger children and move to New Zealand. No headlines at all. The news, if any, will be found underneath a perfume advertisement in very small type. Sometimes it's no more than two or three sentences, and, with any luck at all, you could miss it entirely.

The rest of the paper, however, will be filled with nourishing tidbits. Just last summer I came across a splendid piece that ran under the caption: "Not All Beavers Industrious."

It appears that someone had spent a great deal of time in a beaver community, along with the beavers, trying to discover just how busy they really were. And he did come upon a certain number of upright, responsible beavers who got to the dam on time. On the other hand, there are beavers who loll around all day and never get to the dam at all. And, when they do, they have a couldn't-care-less attitude. They chew indifferently on the wrong kind of twigs and slap mud around carelessly, while taking frequent cat-naps or beaver-naps. They have no group spirit and their work is messy. They are slobs. I hate to say it, but there you are. Nowadays, when *I* loll around, I comfort myself with the thought that I'm just as busy as your average beaver.

I don't want to make it sound as though all were perfection on shipboard. Of course potential hazards lurk everywhere: storms, slippery decks, eccentric people who may sit beside you near the pool. I made one crossing with my deck chair exactly next to the chair of a woman who—

all afternoon, every afternoon—read to her husband aloud from Harold Robbins' *The Carpetbaggers*. While this gave me shooting pains in the back of my neck and caused me to take brisk walks around the deck, which is what I should have been doing anyhow, it was a source of great fascination to the pool attendant, who, clearly, didn't know such things were going on in this world, even in Hollywood.

Something else you may or may not have to deal with is cocktails with the Captain. You may be invited for cocktails because you are a movie star or because you happen to have the same name as the president of the Cunard Line and are mistaken for a relative. In any case, most people make the obvious mistake of trying to be interesting, whereas the Captain is (quite understandably) tired of interesting people. The average Captain, while being as cheery

as a Santa Claus in Macy's, is hardly more articulate. He smiles and smiles and mutters things like "Oh, ho, ho." You can look him straight in the eye and recite the third stanza of *America, the Beautiful* without his perceiving anything amiss. In fact, you can say anything you please so long as you don't make the mistake of referring to his ship as "this boat." This will alert him, and you will then have to listen to a sharp disquisition on the number of significant ways in which a ship differs from a boat. (Billy's *Blue-Jay* is a boat. The *Michelangelo* is a ship. Have you got that now?)

No matter. I want to go down to the sea again. To the lonely sea and the sky. And the nice steward who brings me breakfast to the cabin and the deck steward who tucks a rug around my knees and the good food and the bad movies, and the bingo and the horse-racing, and the salt-spray that makes my hair-do sticky, and the cocktails in the bar as the sun goes down over the ocean, and the telephone in the cabin that never, never rings. I want to go. And I want to go this summer.

What to do when your husband gives up smoking

The best thing to do when your husband gives up smoking is to leave him—just temporarily, of course. He will most surely follow his final cigarette with what appears to be a nervous breakdown, and you may not be able to keep your own cool when all about you this madman is stuffing his face with chocolate covered peanuts, chewing on the horn rims of his glasses, and otherwise behaving like a panther with four sore paws.

Simple efforts to help the victim ("Why don't you calm down, honey?") will go unappreciated. And tempers are prone to rise as the new non-smoker, in a voice rigid with martyrdom, replies, "Boy, that's rich—you sit there puffing away and tell *me* to calm down!" This way lies madness and the marriage that can *not* be saved.

Sneaking your cigarettes in the garage the way the children do is not the real solution. No, the only safe thing to do is clear out of the area for the first week of The Great Experiment. It would be ideal if you could afford to go to Elizabeth Arden's or the Hambletonian Spa from whence you might return so rejuvenated (if not downright catnip) that your husband would be reminded that there was a time in his life when you meant more to him than a cigarette could. If you cannot afford Arden's, remember that your mother in Scranton is always saying how she would enjoy a little visit with you alone sometime.

The reason I didn't leave town for that first week is because I was given no advance warning. It was another one of those cases where the wife is the last to know. On a perfectly ordinary day in February, my husband's part-time secretary called and asked me to give him what I considered a rather cryptic message. When he came home, I passed it on. "Marguerite phoned," I told him, "and she said to tell you *not* to sit at the table after dinner. And do you know what I think? I think you're overworking that nice girl."

"Oh," he explained, "she just means that's when you want one worst." I may have paled as I inquired, "That's when you want one *what* worst?"

Then he made a full confession. He was going to stop smoking beginning tomorrow, and he'd been asking Marguerite for advice because she'd kicked the habit a year earlier. He seemed entirely cheerful about the prospect. In fact, his face was wreathed in smiles. Of course, his face

was also wreathed in smoke from one cigarette in his fingers and another lighted cigarette in the ashtray. But he sounded game as an astronaut ("This voyage to the moon is procedurally routine"). Secretly, all I could think of was Kipling's lament, "Oh, they're hangin' Danny Deever in the mornin'."

The condemned man arose the next day later than usual, because, as he subsequently explained, he couldn't think of any *other* reason to get up. Perhaps I should mention at this point that my husband has always been a serene man. He taught all six children how to tie their shoelaces without once losing his patience. He has been known to go off to his desk humming snatches of *Swanee*. And, what is more to the point, he hasn't been sick one day in twenty years. When he does complain, it's never about his health, but about something important, like "Chicken again? Why don't we ever have anything good, like chili or baked macaroni and cheese?"

Anyway, when I came upon him around noon his desk was a sea of cellophane candy wrappers. Naturally, I asked him how he was managing without cigarettes. He replied that there was no problem about the cigarettes, he was hardly giving them a thought, but his swollen cheeks were bothering him. Furthermore the roof of his mouth felt funny, and what about these strange red marks on the palms of his hands?

I assured him that his face was not swollen and explained that his palms looked exactly as they always did. He just never happened to notice them before. As for the roof of his mouth, I suggested that his consumption of one pound of sour balls in two hours might have something to do with it.

I thought he'd be delighted to learn that all his fears were foolish fancies. On the contrary, he looked forlorn, actually morose. In fact, he hadn't looked so distressed since he finished reading Rachel Carson's *Silent Spring*. I thereupon resolved to treat new symptoms with new respect.

The following day he reported once again that the absence of cigarettes was no problem at all. He didn't even *want* a cigarette. His problem was his eyes. He was very definitely suffering from double vision. I immediately called an oculist, whose nurse explained that it would be six weeks before he could be given an appointment. I begged to speak to the oculist himself and, when he came on, asked if he could possibly see my husband today after office hours. "My dear Madam," he began very impatiently. "But Doctor," I said, "this is an emergency." He asked me to describe the emergency, and I said, "My husband has given up smoking." His whole tone changed. "Of course," he said, "in that case we'll make room for him this afternoon." A humane man—and one who, it developed, had given up smoking five times. There was, of course, nothing the matter with my husband's vision.

Two days later he had a new complaint. His jaws ached and his teeth felt loose, definitely loose. The dentist he consulted could find no sign of any deterioration in the alignment of gum and molar. This surprised me. He had been chewing gum eleven hours a day (two or three sticks at a time) with maniacal fervor, tossing his head from side to side like the M-G-M lion. I thought it likely that he had loosened not only his teeth but his collarbone. It seems that he had never learned to chew gum as a child, and while I know a woman who learned Greek at ninety there are nevertheless some skills, like ballet dancing and gum chewing, which can only be mastered by the very young.

Different people attack the problem of withdrawal symptoms in different ways. I met a professor of economics who told me that after giving up smoking he always kept a child's coiled wire toy—a "Slinky," I believe it's called—on his desk to play with. My husband thought this was an idiotic idea, but I don't know that it's any more idiotic than unbending a bowl full of paper clips and twisting them into tiny nooses, which is what he was doing.

In any case, during this ghastly period I was the perfect portrait of patience, as warm and as wise in my answers as Marmee in *Little Women*. In fact, the whole family was treading as softly as pilgrims in an unfamiliar shrine. Our faithful housekeeper, Mabel, was heard to admonish eight-year-old Gregory. "Don't you throw that ball at the window! Don't you know your father has given up smoking?" When I accepted an invitation to a party I felt it necessary to add, "We'd love to come, but I think you should know that Walter has given up smoking." It wasn't that he was disagreeable or snappish. But he did wear an air of autumnal suffering, like King Lear having just divested himself of his kingdom. And he also gobbled canapés in a manner that six-year-old children would have been rebuked for. Furthermore, it was a problem just to *get* to the party. He would part from his bag of potato chips just long enough to button his dress shirt, the while muttering "Now that I've given up cigarettes, nothing fits me." It was uncanny the way he connected everything that happened to him with the absence of cigarettes in his life. If he passed a red light, it was "Now that I'm not smoking, my reflexes are off." I honest to God think that he believes there was some connection between his giving up smoking and the crisis in the Middle East.

As I've tried to make clear, throughout all of this I remained as vibrantly cheerful as those addled females I see on television who apparently find all happiness here below in a new lemon-flavored furniture polish. Then the day came when I snapped. I found him at his desk looking even more forlorn than was becoming quite usual. Studying his dachshund expression, I was moved to invoke Shakespeare, quoting aloud, "Oh, bare, ruined choir, where late the sweet birds sang."

"It's *not* funny," he said.

"I never said it was funny," I said.

He went on to elaborate. "I haven't mentioned this before, because I didn't want to complain (ho, ho, ho, ho), but I can't work, I can't write, I can't think. And I can't think because my mind is so furry and fuzzy." It turned out that he had had to look up the spelling of the word "neighborhood" because when he'd typed it, it looked peculiar. It wasn't misspelled, it just looked peculiar.

I allowed myself to sound sarcastic. "And I suppose you think it's all because you've given up smoking." "Absolutely," he replied. "Now, honey," I began, "this is ridiculous and you know it's ridiculous—how could not smoking make your head fuzzy?" He looked me straight in the eye and said, absolutely seriously, "I think I'm getting too much oxygen."

That did it. My brusque remarks and clarion tones would have been appropriate coming from a responsible person announcing a fire at sea. But I ask you. A middle-aged man, respected in his field, seriously announcing that his brain is being damaged by breathing in too much unpolluted air!

We have decided to remain together for the sake of the children. And then, too, I have been told that one of these days, when all those noxious tars and resins have finally disappeared from his system, he will be a new man, with new exuberance and new wind. Except that to really appreciate that new wind he will have to lose the eighteen pounds he has gained while giving up cigarettes. And if he gives up eating—no, no, it's too grisly to contemplate.

Why Mommy can't read

One reason I never found myself as a human being is
that I never looked. Actually, I didn't want to know
myself. I'm mixed up enough already, without going into
that kind of thing. Oh, I admit that when I was younger,
and before hope was gone, I was avid to improve myself.
It used to be that when a close friend pulled me into
an alcove and said, "Jean, do you know what your problem
is?" I would always say, "No, what?" Not any more.
For one thing, each of my friends had a completely different idea, and some of the problems I'd never even
heard of. Now I'm firm. I say, "Helen, of course I know
what my problem is, but it hurts me to talk about it."
The surprising thing is that I really do know. My problem
is that I haven't grown.

That I should have found this out was another of those chancy, one-in-a-million things. I was reading the *Sunday News* and happened upon this fascinating article entitled "Why Tony Curtis Switched Love Mates." Just in case you happened to miss it, let me explain that Mr. Curtis had found it necessary to dispense with his first love mate because, according to the article, all the while he was reading good books and going to the Museum of Modern Art *she* wasn't growing at all. I mean it would scare you. And that's when I realized that not only have I not grown these past years, I've shrunk. The proof is that, with a hundred things to do, I would sit there in the middle of the afternoon and read an article called "Why Tony Curtis Switched Love Mates." You can bet your sweet life Curtis doesn't waste his time on that kind of nonsense.

And if the articles I read are hare-brained, the books I read are worse. I don't know how to describe them exactly, but they cost two dollars and ninety-five cents and they have a lot of cartoons. Or when I read a thicker book it always turns out to have been "told" to somebody. And all this time *The Rise of the West* just sits there and sits there. I've even read Helen Gurley Brown's *Sex and the Single Girl*—no, wait, wait, wait, I think I can explain that one.

I was in bed with the flu when I read an advertisement for Mrs. Brown's book. The thing that alerted me was the publisher's statement that "the reader is taken on a guided tour of the haunts of men and told how to flush

them out without doing anything brassy or show-offy."
Even so, I wasn't really a prospective purchaser until
I read, almost last in the bouquet of promises for the
book, "Helen Gurley Brown will teach you how to make
a man glad that he called you on the telephone." Well,
*some*body had better, was my first thought. Of course
I'm not single, I'm not single at all, but nevertheless I do
talk on the telephone and everybody says I'm absolutely
impossible. Actually, I think I know why that is. It's because I never pick up the receiver without being torn between my wish to sound low and musical and my feeling
that I ought to sound like one of the children so that I can
say I'm out in case it should be the school principal
again.

Anyway, I was, as I have said, bedridden, and my husband was going out to the post office. So I said to him, "Honey, on your way back will you pick me up a copy of *Sex and the Single Girl?*" Since he is normally expressionless, I was startled to notice that his jaw dropped open and his eyebrows flew to his hairline.

"You can't be serious," he said, pronouncing each word separately and distinctly like an actor playing Restoration comedy. "You don't honestly expect me to walk into Anderson's bookstore and ask for a copy of *Sex and the Single Girl!*" Suddenly I could see his predicament. But I thought of the solution. "Oh, silly," I said, "you just tell them it's for me." The reasonableness of this was lost on him, and he said, in a voice stiff with irony, "In your opinion, that's *better?*"

"Oh," I said, "never mind, if you're going to be like *that*," and sank back into the pillows, the better to indicate the ravages of my illness. However, a day later he did bring me home a copy. As it turned out, he wasn't embarrassed at all. The salesgirl didn't even notice *Sex and the Single Girl*, buried as it was beneath thirty-two dollars' worth of books on archaeology. This really shows how interested my husband is in me because he certainly isn't interested in archaeology.

But you do see the kind of book I'm reading. I don't know what happened to me. I don't know where it all started. As recently as five years ago I got through *Doctor Zhivago*, and I must say it did have some excellent descriptions of hoarfrost. Furthermore, as a girl I was thought to be deep. I know I will go to my grave be-

lieving that the reason Dickie Grace didn't invite me to the eighth-grade prom was because my mother told his mother that I was reading Emil Ludwig's *Life of Napoleon*. I mean, that's the kind of reputation I really did have. And now look at me.

But things came to something like a head the other night. I was curled up with a Goldenberg Delicious Peanut Chew and a novel that was a best-seller three years ago. (I may read rubbish, but I'm in no hurry about it.) The story was beginning to unfold nicely. The hero (Brad), a Madison Avenue executive, had just turned down a big tooth-paste account because, as he himself put it, "I'm tired of being a dream-peddler." Now he was alone with his secretary, the girl who had always believed in him. "Sharon," he said, "I want out, I want to go back to my roots." Then the two kissed "greedily," which of course was the logic of the situation and the way people really do kiss in novels. But it was right there that the author let me down. In the course of describing the embrace he made reference to Brad's "crisp, black hair" and to Sharon's "moist, red lips." Now even I, mired as I am in the backwash of literature, knew that this was too much. If he was going to have crisp black hair, she simply had to have dry red lips. Or, vice-versa, he could easily have had limp grey hair. But as matters stood I wanted out, I wanted to go back to my roots.

The book dropped from my nerveless fingers as I contemplated that narrow margin of safety that separated me from *Mad Comics*, *Uncle Wiggily*, *Little Golden Books*, *Photoplay*. In panic, I rushed to the bookshelves and fished out the biggest, heaviest, most significant-looking tome I could see, which happened to be Prescott's *The Conquest of Mexico and Peru*. I banished as unworthy my feeling that since I smoke I wasn't likely to live long enough to finish such a lengthy book and started right in with the preface (This in spite of the fact that I know from actual experience that you can skip the preface to *any* book and nobody will ever find out.)

Anyway, I started to read, putting my finger under each word and pronouncing the words aloud. I always do this with a book of any difficulty. It helps to break the ice and catch my attention. With any luck, I get the hang of things in a page or two and am able to proceed in silence.

"As the Conquest of Mexico has occupied the pens of Solis and of Robertson," I began (loudly and clearly), "two of the ablest historians of their respective nations, it might seem that little could remain at the present day to be gleaned by the historical inquirer." I was doing fine. Unfortunately, it was precisely this moment that ten-year-old Gilbert came into the room and we had the following exchange:

"What does it mean not to be taken internally?"

"It means it's poison."

"That's what I told Gregory. I told him to spit it out."

"You told him to spit *what* out?"

"Cloudy ammonia. Why is it cloudy?"

"Good heavens, where is he? How much did he swallow?"

"He didn't swallow any. I just told him to spit it out in *case* he swallowed any."

"And why would you tell him a sappy thing like that?"

"But you just said it was poisonous. He's four years old. He ought to know."

("As the Conquest of Mexico has occupied . . .") But no. I've got to find out for certain where that kid is and where that ammonia is. Ten minutes later I'm back and starting to hunt for the preface again, which is not as simple as it sounds because the table of contents extends for twenty-eight pages. "As the Conquest of Mexico has occupied the pens of Solis" I read aloud, though not quite as loud. But now it's Gregory's turn.

"He hit me. Just because I kissed his ear he hit me."

"You tell him he's not supposed to hit you."

"He knows that. But he hits me all the time."

"That's silly, you know he doesn't. Look, you just tell him if you need to be hit, I'll hit you."

"When?"

"Oh, not now, for heaven's sake! Mommy is reading a book."

"I know. Who is Mexico?"

("As the Conquest of . . .") But Gilbert is there to clarify things.

"Did he tell you that he kissed my ear?"

"That's what he said."

"He bit my ear."

"Well, it doesn't look bit. I mean, I don't see anything."

"That's because it's ear. People don't have much blood in their ear. I just wish he bit my neck, then you'd see how bloody . . ."

"Gilbert, honey, why don't you go look at television?"

147

"Because it's a school night."

("As the Conquest of Mexico has occupied the pens of Solis and Robertson . . .")

"Gilbert, what are you standing there for?"

"I want to see if you're going to read that same thing all over again."

No, I'm not going to read that same thing all over again. I'm going to be very quiet and read a nice story about a young man named Brad who has a secretary named Sharon and crisp, black hair.

Twiggy who?

Actually, I have nothing against Twiggy herself. She seems like a most delightful young boy. Of course, I don't know her personally. I mean, I've never seen her in the almost flesh. But I have seen at least five thousand pictures of her and they do give me pause.

Oscar Hammerstein once wrote a lyric about a girl who was "narrow as an arrow," but of course he was joking. He would never have imagined the day when one of the most popular fashion models in the world would be a girl who called herself Twiggy because she was twiggy.

Well, it's happened, it's a fact and a phenomenon, and I have no intention of railing against it. There are women, you know, who *do* rail. They take one look at Twiggy and blanch and then make sweeping statements like "Well, if Twiggy is In, then I'm Out." Frankly, I think they are lowering themselves. I contain myself and avoid such remarks. In this I am immeasurably aided by the certain knowledge that I wasn't exactly In when Mae West was In, so what does it matter to me who comes and goes?

But I'll tell you who I'm worried about, really worried about. Audrey Hepburn. Compared to present standards, that girl is pretty hefty. And no fooling around about it. Now, what will become of her if she feels driven to compete and tries to "get some of that off?" As it is, she hasn't had a square meal in ten years; you can tell *that* by looking at her. Surely she couldn't subsist on less. And I'd hate to think of that lovely girl perishing. Perhaps her advisers are keeping pictures of Twiggy from her. Let us hope.

Unlike some of my friends (who think Arlene Francis is thin, for heaven's sake), I saw this whole thing coming. I do not go back as far as Lillian Russell, which will surprise my children, but I do remember the friendly forties when we all admired the gorgeously cushioned contours of Ingrid Bergman and miniskirts were worn only by girls under five. And by Scottish bagpipers. It was a great time for a size fourteen to be alive. Even girls who wore size sixteen were taken to dances and occasionally found husbands.

I did not expect this age of felicity to last, and it didn't. I watched the fearful descent from substantial Ingrid to wiry Audrey and finally to Mia Farrow, knowing we were going from pillow to post, and I shuddered. Mia Farrow, for instance, is so worried about every additional

ounce that she's actually chopped off all her hair. (Do you suppose that's why Twiggy pencils in her lower eyelashes? False eyelashes don't weigh much, but they weigh *something*. Well, I have a friend who removes her nail polish before she steps on a scale.)

Anyway, this is what we've come to, here we are, and that's why I think Lynn Redgrave should have won the Academy Award. What Lynn Redgrave was really doing in *Georgy Girl* was making the world safe for larger women. Oh, that splendid big broth of a girl, with yards of hair that she can swing from shoulder to shoulder, and hips, and all the other items that used to be standard equipment before the roof fell in on the fashion industry, or, to be precise, the bottom fell out.

I quite understand that the molders of fashion can't help but be affected by the advent of Twiggy, but I do think

it would be nice if they kept a sense of proportion and re-membered that the rest of us have feelings, too. Just last week a famous Fifth Avenue store ran an advertisement in the *Times* for a dress. "Our cocktail dress," the ad read, "jet-black and terrific. All sizes to ten." Now if they don't want my trade, okay. But what do they mean—*all* sizes to ten? If they're making cocktail dresses for the pre-school group, why don't they say so?

At this point I have a confession to make. I am not the least bit concerned about fashionable clothes because I don't have any. But I *am* concerned about boys because I have five. And, to a boy, they avoid haircuts. They *prefer* to have their hair splashing in their eyes, flopping about their ears, and trickling down the backs of their necks. With the smaller boys, I can take direct action. I stand beside the barber's chair (looking as fierce and intent as a woman in a George Price cartoon) and I say "Pay no attention to this crazy kid, just give him a *regular* haircut." How-ever, with boys who are over six feet tall, the problem is naturally more complicated. To get them to the barber shop requires tact and gentle persuasiveness: "If you come home to this house tonight without that hair gone, I'll kill you." Thus admonished, they do get a haircut, or, rather, they pay a barber a dollar and seventy-five cents to make deli-cate *passados* three inches above their heads. This practice leads to bad jokes: "I said get a haircut, but I meant *all* of them!" It also leads to bad human relations: "Go away. Don't speak to me. I've never met you."

And what, you ask, does this have to do with Twiggy? Something, I think. If the idealized girl is going to look like a boy, then a boy has simply got to look like something else. If it turns out to be an English sheep dog, I guess that can't be helped.

With all the controversy about Twiggy and the explosion of publicity around her it is interesting to notice that some people remain above the storm (above the storm or around the bend, depending on how you look at it). My husband and I were passing the Public Library recently and we saw three teen-age girls sitting on the wall like three sparrows on a branch. They all had crewcuts and wore heavy eye make-up but no lipstick. My husband looked at them and said, "What do you suppose is the matter with those girls?" I explained that I thought they were trying to look like Twiggy. "Twiggy who?" he asked. I launched into an explanation by asking a series of rhetorical questions: "Have you left the planet? Where in heaven's name have you been for the last six months? Do those glasses have to be changed *again?*" He listened with great patience and finally murmured, "Is that so? Now where would I have seen a picture of this girl?"

Once, when the actress Stella Campbell was quarreling with George Bernard Shaw (who was, of course, a strict vegetarian), she turned on him in a fury and exclaimed, "Some day, Joey, you are going to eat one lamb chop and then God help all women!" Well, one of these days Twiggy will discover lollipops and then God help *Vogue* and *Harper's Bazaar*.

The poet and the peasants

We have made mistakes with our children, which will undoubtedly become clearer as they get old enough to write their own books. But here I would like to be serious for a few minutes about the one thing we did that was right. We taught them not to be afraid of poetry.

For a number of years, or until the older boys went away to school, we gathered the protesting brood in the living room every Sunday evening, right after dinner, for what the children scornfully referred to as "Culture Hour." Each boy would recite a poem he had memorized during the week, after which we would play some classical music on the hi-fi for twenty minutes or so. This will sound simple and easy only to those who refuse to grasp that if there is

157

an irresistible force there are most definitely immovable objects.

Actually the program came about by accident. One night I went into the den and turned on a light which promptly burned out. Then when I turned on a second light the same thing happened. Cursing the darkness, I muttered "When I consider how my light is spent . . ."

My husband surprised me by asking, "What's that from?" I recoiled as though he had just announced that he couldn't remember the colors of the American flag. "It's not possible," I said, "that you don't know what that's from. Everybody knows what that's from."

His look was short-suffering. "You don't have to sound so superior," he said. "The first present I ever gave you was a book of poetry." (I was eighteen and it was *The Collected Poems of Stephen Crane*.) "I know that's a poem, I just don't know *which* poem."

"Well," I continued, fatuous as before, "that is Milton's *Sonnet on His Blindness* and it's inconceivable to me that a man who used to be a teacher wouldn't remember." But he had left to get two new light bulbs and out of the range of my voice.

That started me mulling, which is one of the things I do best. Were our five boys going to grow up knowing all about such folk heroes as Joe Namath and Vince Lombardi and nothing whatsoever about Milton or Keats or Yeats or even Ogden Nash? Steps, I felt, had to be taken.

When I first proposed the idea to my husband his enthusiasm was less contagious than I might have hoped. "I don't suppose it will kill them" is what he said. "Them"

at that point were Chris, aged fourteen, the twins, Colin and John, aged ten, and Gilbert, aged seven. There was also Gregory, aged two, who could recite "I love Bosco, that's the drink for me," but I didn't suppose his talents could be pushed further at that juncture.

I did suppose that we could plunge ahead with the four older boys. But if their father felt it wouldn't kill them, they had no such confidence. As I unfolded The Plan they couldn't have been more horrified if I had suddenly suggested that all of them wear hair ribbons to football practice. Nevertheless, I was adamant, and, as it turned out, rather obtuse. At that stage of my life I was still in good voice and bigger than they were. And I was used to giving commands. "Go," I would say to one, and he would goeth, "Come," I would say to another and he would cometh. (Or most of the time he would cometh. Occasionally he would runneth out the back door.)

I always tried (and still do try) to be very specific. To say to a ten-year-old boy, "If you don't start keeping that room tidy, I am going to go absolutely crazy" is a waste of time and breath. To begin with, he doesn't know what the word "tidy" means and he won't find out until he marries the right girl. And since he considers that you are already crazy, he will not believe that his actions are likely to worsen the situation. It may not be infallible, but it surely is more practical to say, "You don't leave this room until I say it is *perfect* and I do mean all those Good Humor sticks under the bed."

Anyway, it was with this sense of being totally explicit that I told the boys one Monday morning, "I want you to find a poem that you like and I want you to learn it so you can say it out loud next Sunday night. Is that clear?" The sighs and the groaning reassured me. I had been prefectly clear. During the week I nudged them from time to time, "How is that poem coming, do you know it yet?"

On Sunday evening there was the usual hassle over whose turn it was to dry the silver and whose turn it was to line the kitchen wastebasket, etc. My own mother used to solve this problem by saying, "Just don't bother, I'll do it myself," but I am too judicious for that and also too lazy. So getting the dishes put away is always a long-drawn-out process. Tonight it was a longer-drawn-out process. But eventually the victims presented themselves in the living room, and the recital began. Three of the boys had selected limericks and poor limericks at that (imagine anybody rhyming "breakfast" with "steadfast") while the fourth recited a lengthy and truly dreadful verse about a Cookie Jar Elf. My husband, more than most men of his generation, has seen some pretty horrendous performances, but this was in a class by itself. He polished his glasses, presumably to make sure that these *were* his children. As for me, I had intended to make a few illuminating comments. Instead I was left as slack-jawed and as speechless as those television commentators who were picked up by the camera minutes after President Johnson announced he would *not* run again.

In the vacuum I put a record, *The Nutcracker Suite*, on the hi-fi and warned the boys they were not to talk, they were to listen. They were not to whisper, they were to listen. The boys kept to the letter, if not the spirit, of the instructions, with the result that I was the one who talked and talked all through the music: "Stop kicking him in the ankle, take that ashtray off the top of your head, I know you can hear the music from there but get out from under the coffee table."

The whole thing was a disaster but, while I was definitely daunted, I was not yet ready to give up. (Remember that *Hello, Dolly!* looked like a failure when it opened in Detroit.) Eventually I was able to identify Mistake Number One. Asking the boys to find a poem they "liked" made about as much sense as asking me to select a Rock Group that I liked. Of course they didn't like poems, any poems. How could they, why should they? When I was the age of our oldest and was required at school to learn whole passages of *The Lady of the Lake,* I thought "The stag at eve had drunk his fill/Where danced the moon on Monan's rill" was pretty ghastly stuff. (To tell the truth, I still think it's pretty ghastly.) Once, as a senior in high school, I got sixty on an English exam because of the way I answered a forty-point question which read: "Discuss Wordsworth's *The World Is Too Much with Us* and explain what it means to you." You will not have to remember the poem to grasp that I was not only saucy but asking for trouble when I wrote that, whatever Wordsworth was looking for as he stood on that pleasant lea, the *last* thing I wanted was to see Proteus rising from the sea or, for that matter, hear old Triton blow his wreathèd horn. I mention this only to make it clear that I was not among those prodigies who are reading Shakespeare's sonnets for pleasure at the age of five. Poetry struck me as an arbitrary and capricious method of avoiding clarity, and where my betters heard lyricism I kept hearing foolishness. If the poem said, "Go, lovely rose!" I found myself thinking "Scram, rose. On the double. Take a powder, rose."

What happened to open my eyes and shut my mouth was quite simple. I was a freshman in college when a Jesuit poet named Alfred Barrett came to lecture. I attended with the same enthusiasm that characterized my presence in Advanced Algebra, sitting way at the back of the hall behind a pillar on the theory that I could live through it if I could sleep through it.

It's hard for me to remember, all these years later, what Father Barrett said about poetry, if indeed he said anything. What he did was to read poetry—some of his own, a great deal of Gerard Manley Hopkins (whose existence I was unaware of), Yeats, Shelley, Donne, and Housman. He read with such clarity, such melody, and, above all, such directness that even I—sixteen-year-old skeptic—was converted on the spot. It wasn't so much that I cried "Eureka—I see!" I felt like a woman I know who swears she didn't get her first kiss until she was twenty-three and who exclaimed, on that occasion, "Hey, why didn't somebody *tell* me?" Later in my life I was to meet a teacher and a director, Josephine Callan, who read poetry even better than Father Barrett did but by that time I was already a believer.

Okay, that was *my* story. To get back to the indoctrination of our boys, it was clear that their taste was decidedly peccable and that we would have to select the poems for them, keeping in mind the difference in the boys' ages. (My husband was quick to point out that fortunately there was no difference in the ages of the twins.) We went through the bookshelves, leafed and leafed, and gave each of the boys a book with the poem he was to learn. This was another error because by the end of the week our good books were dog-eared or rat-eared, depending upon the age and irresponsibility of the boy. For a while after that we typed out copies of the poems, but that was a chore and a nuisance (why is poetry harder to type than *anything?*) so eventually we did in the last place what we should have done in the first place, which was to go out and buy a pile of cheap paperback anthologies (these are widely available and often surprisingly good).

The second, or return, engagement of "Culture" night was hardly an improvement on the first. The fact that the poems were of better quality and somewhat longer made the recitations even more agonizing, if that were possible. The younger boys stared at the rug and mumbled like altar boys answering their first Mass in Latin, while Chris stared at the ceiling and chanted in a loud, dum-de-dum see-saw-Margery-Daw rhythm (banging on every end-rhyme until I could definitely feel my inlays ache.

As I see it now, the surprising thing is that I should have been surprised. Even granting that I was much younger then (I was, you will be able to surmise, over twenty-one), there was no excuse for my being so dim-witted. Did I really believe that we were harboring a gaggle of Laurence Oliviers? (Ellen Terry heard Olivier in a school play when he was eleven and instantly announced, "That young man is already an actor.") Not, heaven forbid, that we were trying to develop actors. In my opinion, young people who wish to become actors have an addiction only a little less dangerous than heroin. No, we didn't want them to qualify for a Tony or an Emmy, we just wanted them to feel at home with language that was different from and better than the colloquial speech they heard every day. We wanted them to accept poetry without embarrassment and perhaps finally to realize that a good poem is an emotional short-cut and not just the long way around.

My husband gave a deep sigh as he faced up to the obvious. "We're just going to have to work on them," he said. And so we did. One week he'd work on two of them while I worked on the other two (the following week we alternated so that the hostility engendered would be evenly divided). Getting a boy and his poem together (a not inconsiderable feat), we read the poem aloud to him, slowly. Ignoring giggles and glassy-eyed boredom, we read it again at the proper speed and then asked questions: What do you think this poem means, is it happy or sad, and so on? Even a piece of verse as simple as "Little Boy Blue" hold mysteries for a seven-year-old. He may not know what the word "staunch" means, or even "musket." Perhaps he may not get the point at all and will be as perplexed as the little toy soldier and the little

166

toy dog as to "what has become of our Little Boy Blue since he kissed them and put them there."

Once we determined that the child actually understood the whole poem, we got *him* to read it aloud, correcting him when he mispronounced words, correcting him when he misread phrases, persuading him not to say the rhyming word louder than any other word in the line. Two of the boys were very quick to grasp inflections; the other two were so slow that rehearsing them was like the Chinese Water Torture and I found myself wondering if there was some way to withdraw from the whole plan—with honor. What kept me resolute was the conviction I read in all those clear blue eyes that I would soon come to my senses, that this madness too would pass.

On the third Sunday night the boys were not exactly ready to cut a tape for Angel Records but they were definitely improved. In fact, the session was almost endurable, and we had some general discussion afterward about what the four poems meant, with even Gilbert making a contribution: "When the angel waked him up with a song it means he was dead, stupid."

Thereafter the Sunday hour became just another fact of life around this house and the boys seemed to accept it with hardly more resentment than they accepted baths or sweaters or my notion that a present that came in the mail required a thank-you letter. And, of course, they did get better. The day finally came when they were really able to tackle a poem without our having to tell them "What Tennyson is trying to say here is . . ." They knew. And if they made mistakes, these were fewer and fewer.

Sometimes they came up with an unusual interpretation that was, we had to concede, quite possibly valid.

But this didn't happen until we'd been through years of poetry, yards of poetry, volumes of poetry. We made a number of discoveries along the way. Christopher in his mid-teens and already a little world-weary had a particular affinity for the cynical or sardonic, whether it was in a simple lyric form like Housman's

> When I was one and twenty
>> I heard a wise man say,
> 'Give crowns and pounds and guineas
>> But not your heart away;
>
> . . . .
> 'Tis paid with sighs a-plenty
>> And sold for endless rue.'
> And I am two and twenty
>> And oh, 'tis true, 'tis true.

or in the rich resonance of Arnold's *Dover Beach:*

> Ah, love, let us be true
> To one another! for the world, which seems
> To lie before us like a land of dreams,
> So various, so beautiful, so new,
> Hath really neither joy, nor love, nor light,
> Nor certitude, nor peace, nor help for pain;
> And we are here as on a darkling plain
> Swept with confused alarms of struggle and flight,
> Where ignorant armies clash by night.

I can still see him—he must have been fifteen, messy and mussed with dirty sneakers and a deplorable shirt—reciting

Browning with all the hauteur and severity of George
Sanders:

> That's my last Duchess painted on the wall,
> Looking as if she were alive. . . .
>   She had
> A heart . . . how shall I say? . . . too soon made glad,
> Too easily impressed; she liked whate'er
> She looked on, and her looks went everywhere.

George Sanders chilled into George C. Scott as he came
to the lines:

> . . . This grew; I gave commands;
> Then all smiles stopped together.

Colin was a very serious ten-year-old (he's now six feet
five and a very serious Harvard junior) and it seemed to
us that he did better with the dark and the dire. "Out of
the night that covers me, black as pitch from pole to
pole," he would say in a voice that was at once sweet
and piercing, "I thank whatever gods may be for my un-
conquerable soul." He was downright threatening as he
recited John Donne's:

> Death, be not proud, though some have callèd thee
> Mighty and dreadful, for thou art not so:
> For those whom thou think'st thou dost overthrow
> Die not, poor Death; nor yet canst thou kill me.

John had a good voice, a trace of ham, and a total lack
of inhibition that made him a natural for the more flam-
boyant ballads. His early pièce de résistance was *The*

Highwaymen by Alfred Noyes. I'm sure he couldn't do it as well today as he could when he was twelve. But then I don't honestly think *anybody* can do *The Highwayman* the way John could when he was twelve. John began the opening lines with a sense of excitement that never flagged:

> The wind was a torrent of darkness among the gusty trees.
> The moon was a ghostly galleon tossed upon cloudy seas.
> The road was a ribbon of moonlight over the purple moor,
> And the highwayman came riding—
>   Riding—riding—
> The highwayman came riding, up to the old inn door.

And he handled the love story of the highwayman and the innkeeper's daughter with great tenderness. Describing how she loosened her hair in the casement window, he would pause before saying, ever so gently, "Oh, sweet black waves in the moonlight!" and then flash with the fire of a prosecuting attorney as the highwayman went

>   Down like a dog on the highway
> And he lay in his blood on the highway, with a bunch
>   of lace at his throat.

With John's passion, one felt that the body was there on the living-room floor. Another of his early hits was *Barbara Fritchie*, and if you think that one is just another chestnut ("Who touches a hair of yon grey head dies like a dog, he said") you haven't heard it read by someone who doesn't *know* it's a chestnut and who believes he was there and is giving you an eyewitness account. John was always awfully good with people who died, or were about to die, like dogs.

Having tried the tried and the true, John gradually moved on to the intricacies of Hopkins, where he could be majestic:

> The world is charged with the grandeur of God.
> It will flame out, like shining from shook foil. . . .

Or filled with righteous indignation:

> Thou art indeed just, Lord, if I contend
> With thee; but, sir, so what I plead is just.
> Why do sinners' ways prosper? And why must
> Disappointment all I endeavor end?

Or rueful, as in *Spring and Fall*, which he recited often because it's a particular favorite of mine:

> Margaret, are you grieving over goldengrove unleaving?
> Leaves, like the things of man, you
> With your fresh thoughts care for, can you?
> Ah! As the heart grows older
> It will come to such sights colder
> By and by, nor spare a sigh
> Though worlds of wanwood leafmeal lie;
> And yet you will weep and know why.
> Now no matter, child, the name:
> Sorrow's springs are the same.
> Nor mouth had, no nor mind, expressed
> What heart heard of, ghost guessed:
> It is the blight man was born for,
> It is Margaret you mourn for.

171

Gilbert, being much younger, was limited to what we thought was "easy," which meant that he got relatively cheerful poems and we got some relief. As I remember it, in his poems he was always planning to go someplace. He was going to see the cherry filled with snow, he was going to go down to the lonely seas again, he was going to arise and go to Innisfree. He was also going to leave Lucasta and go to war, but that was later.

During these evenings we continued to play twenty minutes of music. This became more bearable after I stopped trying to make the boys *look* attentive; it had occurred to me, after many a grinding play and many a dull sermon, that no matter how hard you try *not* to listen, something sticks to you anyway. And some nights we broke the pattern by running the films Leonard Bernstein had made for *Omnibus*. My husband had worked for *Omnibus* and was able to borrow kinescopes of the Bernstein talks on Modern Music, Jazz, The Beethoven Manuscripts, The Art of Conducting, and so on. I think these programs are as exhilarating as anything ever done on television. What the children thought was harder to fathom, since they remained totally noncommittal. Clearly, though, Bernstein made some impression on them. I know this because, months after we had played the last of the series, I discovered that Colin had built a new fort in the backyard. It was a crude affair made from two old card tables, an abandoned playpen, and some tar paper. However, insubstantial as it was, the fort appeared to have a name. A tattered banner floating over the entrance bore the legend: *Fort Issimo*.

172

We also begin to get evidence that gallons of nine-teenth-century poetry hadn't washed over them in vain. I recall one night—the twins were twelve—when John was made an Eagle Scout. Driving home from this awe-inspiring ceremony (oh, the Nobel people could take lessons!), I started to tease John. "Well," I said, "you've reached the top. Now what are you going to do?" The answer came from Colin in the back seat. "Oh," he announced briskly, "I expect he will go down to the vile dust from whence he sprung, unwept, unhonored, and unsung."

Sometimes, I must confess, this readiness with the apt quotation could be quite maddening. I think of another night when the two smaller boys were supposed to have gone to bed but had, against all orders, slipped outside to bat a few balls directly under the living-room window.

Suddenly there was a splatter of broken glass and a baseball on the rug. Chris grinned cheerfully as he said, "Come to the window, sweet is the night air."

During all the years we continued our program I never at any time was given any hint that the boys approved. Not ever, not once. So I was thunderstruck one summer, after they'd all returned from school, when the boys themselves suggested that we resume "Culture Hour" for the weeks they were to be at home. I couldn't have been more startled if they had suddenly volunteered to clean out the attic. In fact, it occurred to me that they were making an elaborate joke (irony is frequently wasted on me), so I pressed for an explanation. It turned out that they thought it was time for Gregory to have "his turn." This might have been taken as further evidence that the older children felt they had been made the guinea pigs of the system while their younger siblings got off scot-free, but here they were volunteering to suffer right along with him. Now I believed them capable of altruism, particularly where Gregory was concerned, but not heroism. It had to be, it just had to be that they enjoyed it.

So we started over with Gregory, who, at seven, was already as complex as John Kenneth Galbraith. Not necessarily smart, you understand, just complex. Some days he'd come bursting in the back door with the air of one who'd just been rescued from a burning building and call out for his father, "Where's Mr. Kerr? I need him." (No, no, no, none of the other boys ever called their father Mister.) The next day he'd drift in as slowly as smoke, like a character out of Chekhov who has just lost his country estates.

Certainly *we* didn't understand him, but he did seem to have certain intimations about himself. Let me explain. On the opening night of the cultural revival, Gregory—with much prompting—struggled and stammered his way through no more than six lines of *The Gingham Dog and the Calico Cat*. It wasn't just that he was confused about gingham and calico. I began to wonder if he knew what dog and cat meant.

I don't remember what the other boys recited that evening, but Chris recited a long section of T. S. Eliot's *Prufrock*. The next morning I was passing through the garage and came upon Gregory building a birdhouse. He was also muttering something to himself. What with the noise of the saw, he wasn't aware that I had come up behind him, so I was able to overhear him. What he was saying, thoughtfully and precisely, was "I am not Prince Hamlet, nor was meant to be."

Soon the summer was over, school began, the Captains and the Kings departed, and the program was dropped. It was never to resume again because the following summer the older boys all had jobs away from home. It was never to resume and something special, I realized, had gone out of our lives. You lose not only your own youth but the youth of your children. Sweet things vanish and brightness falls from the air.

Now all those Sunday nights blur in memory like the ghost of birthdays past. But if there is one night that remains more vivid than the others it is because of my own strange behavior. Colin was just finishing *John Anderson My Jo.* Do you remember it all?

> John Anderson my jo, John,
> When we were first acquent,
> Your locks were like the raven,
> Your bonnie brow was brent;
> But now your brow is beld, John,
> Your locks are like the snaw;
> But blessings on your frosty pow,
> John Anderson, my jo.
>
> John Anderson my jo, John,
> We clamb the hill thegither;
> And monie a canty day, John,
> We've had wi'ane anither:
> Now we maun totter down, John,
> And hand in hand we'll go,
> And sleep thegither at the foot,
> John Anderson, my jo.

I already knew the poem by heart, so how it happened that I heard new meanings in it I cannot exactly explain. All I can say is that after Colin had finished, to the horror of the boys and to my own acute embarrassment, I burst into tears. An uneasy silence prevailed until John said, very quietly, "Mom, it is Margaret you mourn for."

And he was right, you know. He was absolutely right.

My twenty-one minute
shape-up program

I am one of those tiresome people who *will* accept a fifth canapé while protesting to the empty air "I've got to stop eating these things, I'm too fat now." Usually, when my mutterings are overheard, there is some loyal soul at hand to console me. "It's all right," this philosopher says. "You're tall, you can carry it."

I don't know why I have ever allowed myself to be soothed by this observation. When you come to think of it, it doesn't make any sense at all. Carry it *where?* I can't carry it in my two hands in front of me. And all the other places are unsuitable and unbecoming.

However, the day came when a True Friend placed herself between me and a platter of stuffed eggs and said, pleasantly but firmly, "You *are* too fat and I am sending you a copy of *Miss Craig's Twenty-one Day Shape-up Program.* Actually, I knew all about this book because two ladies in my neighborhood who have applied themselves to the text have, in just a couple of months, become so slender and so supple that I'm not sure I quite like them any more.

In any case, my copy arrived last week and the reason I didn't start then is because we had a lot of leftover potato salad to use up. Subsequently we have had houseguests. I can't exercise when I have houseguests. I can't even read the morning paper in the evening when I have houseguests. And since I believe that others may find themselves in this same boat (rocking, rocking and beginning to sink), I have devised my own twenty-one minute shape-up program:

1. *Exercise for the Nose. 2 minutes.* Stand in front of a good mirror. Press your upper teeth down over your lower lip until the entire lower lip is covered with teeth. Lift your nose in the air and wrinkle it until you look rather like a rabbit. Stare at this image for a minute. Now allow your face to relax. You will be forcibly struck with the improvement in your appearance now that you no longer look like a rabbit.

2. *Exercise for Scruffy Elbows. 3 to 5 minutes.* (If you can't tell whether or not your elbows are scruffy, ask somebody.) Cut a lemon in half. Scoop out most of the pulp. Heat a little olive oil in a small saucepan. Pour the oil into the lemon cups. Then rest your elbows in the lemon cups. The whole point of this procedure is to give you a little rest. For, while you are actually in the lemon cups, you can't do anything else whatsoever. You can't even file

your nails, because the least little jiggling will cause the oil to ooze out all over the table. If one of the children comes in and asks you what you are doing, refuse to answer. For those who worry about such things, I have been assured that this exercise is in no way injurious to the elbows.

3. *Facial Mask for Toning Up the Complexion. 4 minutes, 30 seconds.* Make a facial mask with one cup of butterscotch ice cream and three tablespoons of baby oil. (The purpose of the baby oil is to keep you from licking the ice cream.) Apply this liberally all over the face. (You may wish to use rubber gloves because it's pretty cold.) Stand close over a sink, because it does drip. After the ice cream

has completely melted off your face (the time varies with the heat of the bathroom), rinse your face with lukewarm water and clean up the floor. This should be very beneficial for your circulation. And, what is more to the point, after several applications you will find that you no longer wish to eat ice cream in any flavor, which certainly is a step in the right direction.

4. *Exercise for Abdomen and Upper Arms. Time: I'll just have to give you some leeway here, it could take all day if you're unlucky.* Find an old bathing suit that is a size too small for you. If it should turn out that your new, or current, bathing suit is a size too small for you, you will of course save the time it takes to hunt all over the attic for an old one. Put on the bathing suit. And—this is important—do not get any help in closing the zipper. There is no exercise so efficacious for the upper arms as the effort involved in closing the back zipper of a tight bathing suit. Many women report that before they complete the last five inches of the zipper they are gasping heavily. This is understandable and also very good for the upper abdomen muscles. If you have any doubt about this, just place your hand gently on your upper abdomen and give a loud gasp. You will sense that the abdomen is definitely doing something.

5. *Exercise for the Upper Thigh. 4 minutes and not a second longer.* Holding firmly to the two sides of the refrigerator, raise your right leg behind you until it forms a right angle with your body. Now raise it higher still until the whole leg throbs. Repeat, using left leg. Continue this exercise until you have reached the state of mind where it

is perfectly clear to you that you would prefer to have flabby legs rather than put yourself through this kind of thing. Now, open the refrigerator and make yourself a small snack, which you are certainly entitled to. And, speaking of snacks, do you find it as heartening as I do to know that even chocolate milkshakes are not so high in calories or so fattening as an equal amount of codliver oil? Once you have grasped that fact, you will not keep loose bottles of codliver oil lying about the house.

10 *Minute Reading Interval*. Early in the week tear out of newspapers and magazines articles which you judge to have a special interest for you. *I* gravitate to those pieces which remind me that I am not the only person in this world who has problems. For instance, a piece that made me more willing to hoe my own lonely row came from a British weekly. It was captioned "Liz and Burton Plagued with Problems as They Refurbish Yacht." Now those who have never tried to decorate a yacht will make light of the difficulties, but I assure you it was hell. The paneling, brought over piece by piece from Florence, didn't fit. Workmen dropped a large onyx table on the gangplank and it was badly chipped. (The table; God knows what happened to the gangplank.) Worst of all, the inlaid carpeting had been entirely installed when it was discovered that the manufacturer had forgotten to have it Scotch-guarded or Welsh-guarded or whatever it is you do to make the world safe from irresponsible terriers.

This last oversight was discovered, or—to be more explicit—revealed, by one of the Burton dogs short minutes after the last carpet tack was nailed down. I am eagerly awaiting the follow-up story. Did the Burtons get rid of the carpeting or the dogs? (One supposes they made the usual compromise and simply rearranged the furniture.)

Another item that brought me cheer was a short piece that appeared in our local newspaper. "Heart Attacks Rare Among the Mentally Ill," the headline ran. Reading on eagerly, I learned that mentally ill persons are not sufficiently well organized to react to stress. Being unable to grasp what a mess we're all in, they do not worry. And it is this lack of worry that reduces heart strain. You didn't know that, did you? However, the mentally ill *are* subject to respiratory ailments. The article doesn't say why, but I assume that mentally ill persons just don't have sense enough to come in out of the rain. Now you will wonder why I take heart from this theory, or why, indeed, I identify with mental cases. I'll tell you. The simplest definition of a mentally ill person is—to me—the most acceptable: i.e., a person who does not function properly in the environment, "one who does not cope." I do not cope. Of course, I cope every so often, but there are whole days, even weeks, when my behavior is, to put the best face on things, eccentric. Last Monday it took me two hours to find my car in the parking lot in front of Korvette's in Scarsdale. One reason for this is that Korvette's has an enormous lot. Another is that I was looking for a beat-up white Chevvy whereas, it turned out, I was that day driving a beat-up brown Buick. This became clear as the store closed and the other cars drove away.

I also got very wet, as a sharp rain started up during my search. Knowing myself to be subject to respiratory ailments, I decided to take a hot bath and hot toddy when I returned home. But first I set the oven to 325 and put in the leg of lamb for dinner. I returned to the kitchen two hours later, feeling much restored, and found that I had neglected to turn the oven *On* to *Bake*. Do you see why I feel so certain that I will never have a heart attack?

End of Reading Interval. It's good to stretch the mind as well as the body once in a while.

6. *Exercise for the Will Power. Time: 1 minute for every 10 pounds you are overweight, considering 4 minutes as an absolute ceiling.* Still wearing that tight bathing suit, stand in front of a full-length mirror. Turn so that you are in profile. Lower your chin until it almost reaches your collarbone. Let your arms dangle. Allow the stomach muscles to sag completely. (Your average stomach muscle is only too willing to sag even without permission.) In this sorry posture, gaze into the mirror until tears of self-pity actually begin to well up in your eyes. Some women will be reminded of those last troubled weeks before the twins were born. I myself think of a horrendously overendowed Samoan woman whose picture appeared in an early issue of the *National Geographic*. Remember when you were a size 12, and everybody said you looked just like Loretta Young? (Oh, time, go backward in your flight!)

But never mind the past. You are here eyeball to eyeball with reality. And there is no use recriminating. You've got to change the menu. Of course it is easier and cheaper to feed the kids what they really like, which is spaghetti and macaroni and chili and lasagna and large leaden cheeseburgers brought in from a roadside stand. But your path

185

lies elsewhere. Are you a woman or are you a mouse? Are you a molehill or are you a mountain? All right, we're not going to cry and we're not going to panic. We're going to take steps and not be like those women who, as my husband says, watch their weight constantly. They don't do anything about it, they just watch it.

7. *Exercise to Restore Lost Nerve. Time: add up all previous times and subtract them from the basic 21 minutes; if you find that you are already over 21 minutes, so do I.* Remove that ghastly bathing suit and put on a garment that is a lot too big for you. Any old maternity dress is good for the purpose. And if you can't find one, put on your husband's bathrobe. If his bathrobe *isn't* a lot too big for you, I am afraid you are in deep trouble and I don't think I can help you. I don't think even Miss Craig can help you. You get a little of that weight off and come back to see us then.